There's No Prereq for Home Ec!

Gloria Humphreys

Copyright © 2024 Gloria Humphreys
All rights reserved
First Edition

PAGE PUBLISHING
Conneaut Lake, PA

First originally published by Page Publishing 2024

ISBN 979-8-89157-976-7 (pbk)
ISBN 979-8-89157-989-7 (digital)

Printed in the United States of America

To all the home economics/FCS teachers past, present, and future

CONTENTS

Introduction vii

Chapter 1: Becky Homecky 1
Chapter 2: Accepting the Challenge 2
Chapter 3: The Journey Begins 4
Chapter 4: A Lesson in Racing 6
Chapter 5: All Buttoned Up 8
Chapter 6: As the Pages Turn 10
Chapter 7: Sew Much Fun! 13
Chapter 8: The Games We Play 16
Chapter 9: Yakety Yak…Please Talk Back! 19
Chapter 10: Hired or Fired? 28
Chapter 11: My Hat Collection 33
Chapter 12: Moving to the Mitten 40
Chapter 13: I Must Have Been Absent That Day 44
Chapter 14: The Grocery Getter 48
Chapter 15: Sex Ed…You Just Had to Be There! 54
Chapter 16: "Seam"ingly Funny 58
Chapter 17: Opposites Attract 60
Chapter 18: S'more Hunting 62
Chapter 19: A Labor of Love or Hell's Kitchen? 64
Chapter 20: Lost and Found 69
Chapter 21: All Cracked Up 72
Chapter 22: "Where There's Smoke…or *Not*" 74
Chapter 23: The "Wig" Raising Student 76

Chapter 24: The Sin Bin 78
Chapter 25: Part 1: Sewcial 82
            Part 2: Distancing 85
Chapter 26: Rewind or Unwind? 88
Chapter 27: The Misfits 89

Acknowledgments 95

INTRODUCTION

When I tell people I am a Family and Consumer Sciences (FCS) teacher, many have no idea what that means, so I say, "It used to be called home economics…" and before I can say anything else, I often hear, "It's a shame they don't teach those skills anymore." That is my cue to explain that what we do now is so much more than just *'stitchin'* and *'stewin'*; which usually gets a laugh, but it's a great opportunity to explain that we still teach those important skills but with a new perspective. I tell them I provide situations or scenarios that force students to demonstrate employability skills; such as teamwork; problem-solving; reading and writing; communication; organizational, mathematical and critical thinking. Some responses I get are "Wow, I never thought of home ec like that." or "It's good to know those skills are still being taught." If time permits, I can explain one or two of my favorite projects—*Teen Living, Inc, My First Kitchen, Yakety-Yak* or *The Little Kitchen*.

Another common question that comes my way is "Why did the name change? Nobody knows what FCS is!" My brief explanation is that factors in our society have changed the "look" of families, individuals and the workplace. Therefore, the curriculum needed an updated perspective in order to meet evolving needs; so in 1994, home economics was changed to Family and Consumer Sciences. (AAFCS.org)

If you are old enough to use the term home economics as a course you took in high school, then you probably remember an additional component known as Future Homemakers of America

(FHA). In 1999, the FHA organization was renamed Family, Career and Community Leaders of America (FCCLA) as a Career and Technical Student Organization (CTSO) and is an integral part of the FCS education curriculum.

Through participation in competitive events, becoming involved in community service opportunities, student leadership, and attending leadership conferences, members develop real world skills, explore career pathways, and become college-and-career ready in addition to strengthening personal life skills such as planning, goal setting, problem-solving, decision making, and interpersonal communication. FCCLA is *not* a club, it's a leadership adventure! Did you know that Dolly Parton, Reba McEntire, Deborah Norville, Bo Jackson, George Clooney and Herschel Walker are among some FHA/FCCLA alumni? (fcclainc.org,wa-fccla.org)

I do not know of any school district whose mission statement is to graduate irresponsible young adults who will become a burden to society. In fact, most mission statements don't even mention specific courses. Instead they encompass the idea of helping students transition from high school into the world of work as well-rounded individuals. Family and Consumer Sciences classes and FCCLA do just that by providing authentic experiences, integrating various types of relationship skills, making responsible decisions and demonstrating practical problem solving. So the next time you think of home economics as the '*stitchin*' and '*stewin*' class—think again.

CHAPTER 1

Becky Homecky

I KNOW HOME ECONOMICS IS NOW REFERRED to as Family and Consumer Sciences, but that didn't make for a great book title. So for the purpose of this book, I'll be using "home ec." Besides, my nickname in college was "Becky Homecky."

There's No Prereq for Home Ec! was an idea that came about a few years ago when I was complaining to a staff member about how my students are coming to class with fewer and fewer "common sense" skills. Each year, it seems students are lacking skills that were once thought to be "common knowledge," and so every fall, I ask myself, *What is going to be missing this year?* This book is not really about skills needed or skills lacking for home ec, but it is about my thirty-plus years of experience as a home economics teacher.

The inspiration for becoming a home economics teacher was my grandmother, Bertha Humphreys. She taught home economics in the Philadelphia Public Schools from about 1927 to 1965. I always wanted to follow in her footsteps, so in August of 1992, I graduated with my Bachelor of Science degree in Home Economics Education from Louisiana Tech University and started my journey. And what a journey it has been. The stories and experiences I write about are based on true situations. Many stories are funny, but some are serious and, in some cases, sad.

CHAPTER 2

Accepting the Challenge

IN THE EARLY '90S, APPLYING FOR A teaching job was quite the experience—no Google, no LinkedIn, no Zoom, and definitely no cell phone interviews. If I did receive a phone call, it was done via a landline, and if I missed a call, the game of phone tag was sure to ensue. The application process took a lot of work and time because I couldn't just create electronic files and upload them to each district. I had to submit a typed application, literally I had to use a typewriter which made me think of this: the first time I saw my mom's typewriter was in 1982 when I needed to type my senior term paper. I asked her, "How do you plug this in?"

She laughed and said, "There isn't a plug because it is not electric."

I probably looked at her with bewilderment much like a millennial doing the rotary phone challenge. Thank goodness by 1992 we had upgraded to an electric typewriter.

In addition to the traditional portfolio items, many of the districts I applied to required applicants to include a detailed lesson plan with visual aids, assessments, and a classroom management plan. To make things more difficult, I was finishing up my student teaching at Crowville High School in Crowville, Louisiana, about ninety minutes away from Ruston, Louisiana, where I lived. My father was a professor in the School of Business at Louisiana Tech University, and he was the one who convinced me to try college again. The first go-round of college didn't go so well for me, and my father knew I was unhappy in Virginia trying to make sense of my life. I was unsure if I wanted to live with my parents, but I am so grateful I did because those years were some of my best memories. I fell in love with this whole college experience and was grateful that it ended on a high note.

While I continued the job search, I was in the process of moving back up to Virginia, so to make it easier on myself, I hired a headhunter. I remember feeling overwhelmed by the whole process but excited at the same time because I was ready to start my "career," not my job. Within a few weeks, I had my first interview with the Montgomery County Public Schools in Virginia where I was offered a one-year contract as the home economics teacher at Shawsville High School. I had no idea what to expect as a brand-new teacher, but I knew the opportunity would be fun, exciting, and educational…I just had no idea how "educating" it would be.

CHAPTER 3

The Journey Begins

My classroom was divided into three basic sections: a classroom, a dining room, and a kitchen that had five lab stations, each equipped with the standard appliances, including dishwashers. Unbeknownst to me, a student had started the dishwasher before joining in the classroom activity. A bit later, I looked toward the kitchen and took a double take because I wasn't sure what I was seeing. Against the glass windows and door were bubbles crawling upward toward the ceiling. I honestly can't remember what I said verbatim, but I do know that somewhere in my response was "At least the whole kitchen is clean." It was also the moment when everyone learned firsthand that liquid dish soap is *not* the same as dishwasher detergent. This incident was my first "funny" teaching experience but definitely not my last.

Several weeks later, I walked into class to find about one-third of the students absent, and I wondered why. I was informed that many students were absent because the opening day of hunting season was basically a "sanctioned" holiday. I was not familiar with the sport of hunting and had no idea how important hunting was to my students. I grew up in Richmond, Virginia, and the closest thing to hunting for me was the fake gun I twirled as a member of the Monacan High School Honor Guard team.

Once the majority of the students were back in class, I planned a food demonstration because I knew that would keep their attention, at least for a bit. As I was prepping, one of the boys asked, "What are you making?"

I said, "Chocolate mousse."

To my surprise, he was completely disgusted as he said, "Why would you put chocolate on moose?"

After some laughter from the class, I said, "My mousse is a dessert, and it never had antlers."

Years later, I would have another group of students who were avid hunters, and I will share those stories in chapter 18, "S'more Hunting."

Like most teachers, the theme of my first year was *survival*, and so that was how I made it through to the end of the year but not before I got into some serious hot water with the principal. My sewing class had been working on a lengthy project, so I entered an "Incomplete" for the report card grades. I was never told I can't "do this," but the principal straightened me out right away by calling me at my home (rut ro), and he was not happy. I apologized immediately and fixed the situation the next day by moving the project into the next marking period. Recalculating grades was not an easy task because there were no systems like Power School, Schoology, Pinnacle, etc. to use, so I had to figure grades using a calculator!

In my experience, home ec teachers are "asked" to host various events for school, especially at the last minute and on a shoestring budget; and my first hosting experience was a basketball tournament for several coaches, referees, etc. I served heavy hors d'oeuvres, so the food could be eaten quickly. I thought things were going well until I opened the Crock-Pot; to my horror, the meatballs had turned green. At first I panicked, thinking they "went bad" but quickly realized that when you mix grape jelly with yellow mustard, you get a green sauce. I made sure I explained that to the guests so no one would think I was trying to kill them. By the way, they were delicious.

CHAPTER 4

A Lesson in Racing

AT THE END OF MY FIRST YEAR, I moved back to Richmond where I continued teaching ten more years before moving to Michigan. I was hired by Henrico County Public Schools as a traveling FCS teacher between JR Tucker High School and Byrd Middle School. I began my day at JR Tucker High School teaching an independent living class for juniors and seniors.

During the career unit, each student had to research a career and create a portfolio for a mock interview. I had one student, Marcus, who wanted to be a professional race car driver and was extremely frustrated with the whole process. I tried to help engage him as best I could, but I was still learning the ropes and was not as wise as I am now.

After discussing appropriate attire, handshakes, and questioning, the students were ready to show off their skills. The interviews were going great until it was Marcus's turn. His situation stumped me because I was clueless as to how I could relate to his choice of a career. When he came to the interview area, he was disheveled, lacking eye contact, and his body language basically screamed, "I am not down with this." I was honest with him and told him I was at a loss for how to have an interview for this specific career, so I asked him to explain what it takes to become a professional driver. As he told me, he brightened up, was more enthusiastic, and he truly believed he would fulfill his dream. As I listened to him, I thought of an idea so he could demonstrate the skills I was looking for, so I asked him about getting sponsors.

After listening, I said, "Okay, I am going to pretend to be a sponsor, and you are going to convince me that you are a worthy investment."

His interview was amazing. He was focused and engaged, kept eye contact, sat up straight, and gave me a handshake at the end—a good, firm one, not the limp fish one. I don't know what happened to him after that year, but I remember how "stupid" I felt because I thought, *I can't help this kid because our worlds are too far apart.* But isn't that what teaching is about, closing gaps and building bridges?

CHAPTER 5

All Buttoned Up

The rest of my day was spent at Byrd Middle School where I worked with sixth-, seventh-, and eighth-grade students. The sixth-grade students were part of an exploratory wheel, which meant the class stayed together as they rotated each nine weeks between wood shop, art, language, and home ec. I really liked this concept because I got to know a lot of students and was able to tell them about elective classes for their seventh-grade year.

If you've ever taught sixth grade, you can relate to the fact that many of them are very straightforward and don't really hold back on what they want to say. One day, I was at the chalkboard—yes, the old-fashioned one—writing, and this young man raised his hand to get my attention. I said, "Hang on, I'll get to you in a minute."

Well, I didn't get back to him as fast as he would have liked, so he interrupted me again. I repeated my response but was more terse this time. On his third try, he just bypassed the politeness of raising his hand and loudly said, "Ms. Humphreys, your dress has popped open!"

I felt my face go red as I looked down quickly to see how much I was "exposing" and gauging how much therapy these little people might need from seeing their teacher in her underwear! Luckily, I had worn a slip, so only minimal damage was done. I thanked him and apologized for not listening sooner. At that point, I completely forgot what I was supposed to be doing, so we played four corners and 7-Up for the last bit of class; some days you just have to do what you have to do. I am not sure how they told their parents what happened because once kids quit bringing home the artwork for the fridge, they apparently do nothin' all day at school on the taxpayer's dollar.

Sixth graders say the darndest things. Another sixth-grade funny experience happened because I received a beautiful floral arrangement from my boyfriend. Of course, the students began to ask all kinds of questions, like "Who are they from?" "Do you have any pictures of him?" etc. As I was answering some of their questions, I overheard two boys talking. The one turned to his shoulder partner and said, "I bet he's going to do something bad and he's apologizing in advance." He was so serious, and I couldn't hold back my smile, but I found myself wondering how he came up with "that" response; it seemed so grown up for sixth graders. Ummm.

One day, my mom, her best friend, my sister, and my nephew stopped by to visit. I introduced them, and, of course, my mom was introduced as Mrs. Humphreys. They then spent a few minutes walking around and talking to the class. As they were leaving, one of the students said, "I never thought about teachers having parents." That made my mom chuckle.

CHAPTER 6

As the Pages Turn

MY SECOND YEAR IN HENRICO COUNTY, I was able to be full-time at Byrd Middle School because a reading class was added to my schedule. Each grade level had a different type of reading focus for the first forty-five minutes, and then everyone had forty-five minutes of study hall. Hopefully, this personal journal entry I wrote will provide some insight into what we did in class.

January 21, 2000

I have had the opportunity to teach seventh-grade reading for several years since I have been at Byrd. A tradition in my class has been a read aloud of Flight #116 Is Down, *which is an adventurous book written by Caroline B. Cooney. One year, I arranged for a local EMS/rescue squad team member to speak to my class about the things they learned from reading the book. The book is about a 747 that crashes on an estate. The only family member at home at the time of the incident is Heidi, a sixteen-year-old who feels as if she can never amount to anything or ever do anything right. When the plane crashes, Heidi jumps into action and begins to handle situations she never thought possible.*

As the rescue workers arrive on the scene, Heidi realizes that there are many junior EMTs—people her age who are trained to handle crisis-related situations. As she works with these people, she realizes that she can accomplish "things" and that most importantly, she became "helpful."

The book describes, in a fair amount of detail, the plane crash scene, the injuries, the condition of the plane, and the condition of the passengers who are alive but trapped. The detailed description allows the reader to gain a greater understanding of the whole problem. Once the rescue workers have arrived, the appropriate command stations are set up and the rescue effort begins.

When Captain Lange, Henrico Fire & Rescue, came to speak to my class, he had students play various roles in a mock mass casualty scene. We had a triage staging area, main command center, transportation center, and, of course, the injured who were tagged according to their injuries.

This activity allowed the students to experience some of the emotion and adrenaline that the characters had exhibited. Captain Lange also gave the students an assignment—they were to pretend that a mass accident occurred here on the Byrd Middle School campus. They were to set up a command center, a triage staging area, and a plan for transporting the injured. When the students returned their diagrams, I was very impressed with their problem-solving skills and believe everyone enjoyed the activity, and I plan to do it again in the future.

Around 1997, I was given an eighth-grade reading class. The reading structure for this class was forty-five minutes of silent reading and then forty-five minutes of study hall. This was the time when the Harry Potter books came to the market and were a favorite choice for many students. I did not have a problem with any of the students except one. He was a tough nut to crack, and I had to get creative with him. He was a sullen student who clearly did *not* want to read at all, but it was my job to get him engaged. I had just finished reading *Watchers* by Dean Koontz and really thought he would like the book. However, due to the nature of the book, I did not feel comfortable letting him do that without parental and administrative approval. I knew our assistant principal had just read the book, so I told him my dilemma and my solution. He was completely on board, so I called the parent right away and explained my idea. She gave the green light, and the rest is history. I don't remember the student's name, but he dove into that book and became a fan of all the Dean Koontz books. Needless to say, the silent reading was no longer a struggle for him. I often wonder if he kept reading for pleasure.

CHAPTER 7

Sew Much Fun!

FOR THOSE OF YOU THAT HAVE TAUGHT any sewing classes, you know there is joy and pain that comes with this particular experience. I have a few stories about sewing that I hope you find at least somewhat humorous.

During one of the sixth-grade sewing projects (a felt tic-tac-toe board), a young man decided it would be funny to put his finger in the center tube of a large spool of thread. What was not so funny was that he could not get it out. I thought about pouring oil all over his hand but figured that wouldn't work. I did, however, remember that his mom worked in the cafeteria, so he and I took a little walk. He was nervous because he was afraid his mom would be "really" mad at him, but when she saw what happened, she burst out laughing. I did not take him to his mom to embarrass him, but I needed her permission so I could have the spool sawed off by the shop teacher. Everyone within hearing distance was now laughing and in some cases crying. The finger and child survived, but the spool of thread perished. I should have given him the remnants of the spool as a "reminder" of why thinking before doing is a great approach to most things in life.

The next story is just one "you had to be there for." Managing a sewing class is whatever works for the teacher. I tried multiple strategies, such as having the students write their names on the board or put a red plastic cup at their station as a way of "flagging" me for help. None of those worked for me because I spent most of the time running around fixing the same problem over and over. That is when I came up with the strategy that worked from that day forward. I decided I would sit in one place and have the students form a line to see me. This allowed me to help without a lot of distractions and at the same time the students in line often had their own question answered by hearing what was being said. If a student needed me to go to the machine, I did while the rest of students in line stayed there until I was back on my perch. Little did I know that my new method would create one of my all-time "Are you kidding?" stories.

One day, I was sitting on my stool helping students, and everything seemed to be going as planned. The student I had just helped turned to go back to his seat when the student directly behind him pulled the kid's pants down. Unfortunately, the underwear came down with the pants, showing the entire male genitalia. There was a huge gasp, and I looked up to see one of my female students heading my way with her eyes as big as saucers.

I asked her, "What happened?"

She said, "I saw it all."

And I asked, "Saw all what?"

As she tilted her head in the direction of the two boys, I realized what had happened. I was mad as a hornet, and with my teacher "hands on the hip" stare down, everyone remained quiet as I asked someone to get the assistant principal who was just two doors down. I took the offender out into the hall and told Mr. Sukonick that I couldn't give the details at the moment because I had to wrap up class. Sewing cleanup takes a bit more time than usual; however, the truth was I was buying some time so I could take a breath and figure out my next move. I checked in with the "victim," and he said he was fine; I checked in with "the bystander," and she said she was okay as well.

Once I calmed down, I began writing the administrative referral, which was not easy. After writing the referral, I took it to the assistant principal so he and I could sit and talk about what happened. He began reading and seemed puzzled, so he asked me something, like "Is this for real?" I assured him it was because my mind was still swirling. He then commented on how delicate this situation was and he was not sure how he was going to explain the details to the "offender's" parents, the "victim's" parents, or the "bystander's" parents. I told him that's above my pay grade and wished him well as I left his office.

CHAPTER 8

The Games We Play

IN MY FIRST INTERVIEW AT BYRD MIDDLE School, I was asked by the principal, Dr. Ware, if I'd be willing to coach soccer. The district was starting a girls soccer team, and from my résumé he saw that I played coed soccer in high school. I am a new teacher looking for a permanent job, so I was not going to say "No, I don't think so," but I wasn't going to tell him that I knew jack—— about coaching. But it's middle school, so how hard can it be? I accepted the challenge very eagerly and very quickly. Mrs. Stanley was the current FCS teacher in the interview, and she gave Dr. Ware, the teacher "look."

He said, "I am not concerned with her ability to teach, you can teach her the ropes, but I need someone to coach the girls." Little did I know, I would be modeling Ted Lasso's approach to coaching—players before points.

Once the team was selected, I made my expectations very simple—school comes first. This expectation was not a problem until one of the top players was given a detention; I did not care if it was before school, after school, or at lunchtime, I was holding my ground and benched her for the next game. That game was one of our rival opponents, and I received pushback from my assistant coach, the players, and, of course, some parents. I reminded the players that they knew my expectations when they made the team, and I was not lowering them. I told the players that our success had come from teamwork and not that of one individual player. The game was exciting, and more than once, my assistant coach begged me to put her in, and I would not. In the last twenty seconds of the game, the center forward kicked from center field and scored the winning goal! It was one of my best and favorite memories not because we won but because I held my ground. I did get apologies from my assistant coach, the team, and a few parents.

This next soccer story was quite different. My players had a lot of talent because they had been playing soccer for years and were on travel teams. Needless to say, they didn't really learn any new skills or drills from me, but they did learn to appreciate the sport from another perspective. There was only one team that I did not like to play, and that was because the skill levels of the two teams were on opposite ends of the spectrum. My players had been kicking soccer balls for years, whereas the opponents may have kicked a ball for the first time at the tryouts. The very first time we played them, I didn't really understand all the dynamics of this whole (soccer) thing, so when we beat them by double digits (24–0), I was happy for our players but felt bad for the opponents. The next day at school, I was called to the principal's office and was informed of the "slaughter rule"—that didn't really exist, but I got his point. He called the other school's principal to apologize.

The next time we played them, I let the game begin in the usual fashion, and after we had scored two goals in a matter of minutes, I called time-out and had a little talk with the referees. I told them my plan, and they looked intrigued, so they gave me the thumbs-up—after all it was just middle school. I talked to the other coach and told her I wanted to even up the teams—I would give her half of my girls and she would give me half of hers. She did have a few really strong players, but they could not carry the team. She was delighted and the switch began. My players were *not* happy with me, but they knew to respect my decision. The parents weren't happy either, but I did not care because this was about the girls. We still won, but that didn't seem to bother the other team because they had so much fun playing the game like it was "supposed" to be played. Afterward, we were applauded and thanked because that was the first time the opposing team's parents did not dread watching their daughters get run over. I had a lot of good memories and good games during my six undefeated years of "coaching" soccer.

CHAPTER 9

Yakety Yak…Please Talk Back!

THIS CHAPTER IS ABOUT THREE OF MY all-time favorite projects. "Yakety-Yak" was my first favorite project that I designed for my sixth graders. The students created a board game using poster board, magic markers, scissors, rulers, and electrical tape. That might not seem like a big deal to some people, but this project forced students to demonstrate various employability skills, such as following directions, meeting deadlines, practical problem-solving, critical and creative thinking, accepting responsibility, and being accountable, just to name a few.

Students had to follow some basic guidelines for the board setup, but then they could stretch their imagination. Each student had to decide the rules of his/her game and write them out in a logical step-by-step manner and then ask two peers to review the rules to see if they made sense. Peer review was important in various ways, and my goal was to have students give specific feedback, not "that's great" or "looks nice," etc. I wanted the students to process the information and come up with a valid response. Forcing the students to interact one-on-one with peers could also be a bit awkward because not all students knew everyone in the class, so the requirement was to select a peer they knew and a peer they did not know well. I always assigned this project at the beginning of the nine weeks because it provided a great opportunity to create some interaction and get to know each other, me included.

Once the project was complete—board, cards, rules, pieces, etc.—they had to sit down and play the game, with their family, without distractions. This was before the cell phone addiction, but there were still challenges. Trying to get a family of five of varying ages to sit down and play a game that was made by a sixth grader was not always an easy sell. However, the comments I received from the parents and the students were priceless. As we were discussing how the activity went, a student commented that playing the game made it easier to talk about uncomfortable things, like grades, and they saw different sides to family members, especially when they had to do something funny like sing and use a broom as a microphone or acting out how a "Grabby Bug" acts in a restaurant.

Below I have listed the six categories for the cards and have given some examples so you can see how the questions required participation from each family member. Most parents wrote raving reviews of the assignment for many reasons. One family had younger children, and the fact that the game was "kid-friendly" made it easy to include everyone. Other parents said how fun it was to make a fool of yourself in front of your children, without embarrassing them in front of their friends. The majority of the students said it was fun to make the board because they got to talk to their friends in class and get treats from me. In all the years I did this activity, I only had one parent who thought the game was a waste of time, but I was not worried because my principal backed me 100 percent.

As I was typing in the examples below, I read the card about waiting to use the phone and laughed because today's kids wouldn't get "it."

Yakety-Yak…Please Talk Back! Sample questions			
Giving Guidance and Support	Should you ever quit going to your parents for guidance? Why or Why not?	You didn't go to your brother's soccer game as he had asked you to do. Go back to the nearest "Guidance" square.	Why is it important to seek guidance when you're faced with a problem you don't know how to handle?

Just for Fun	Talk about one of your bad habits…don't be long-winded!	Give one word to describe each person in the group.	What TV or movie star would you like to invite to your birthday party? Why?
Sharing Responsibilities	You forgot to walk Spot. Spot wet the rug. Go back to the nearest "Responsibility" Square.	Name a right and responsibility that relates to family relationships.	Name two responsibilities you have as a member of this family. What would happen if you did *not* carry out your responsibilities?
Making Decisions	You passed too near your father's brand-new car and scratched it with your gym bag. What are you going to do about this situation?	You get cut from the soccer team. How would you handle the rejection? Give three possible examples.	On Halloween, you are with a crowd of people who pull up all the flowers in crabby Mrs. Jones's flower bed. Should you do anything about this situation or not? Explain.
Communicating Effectively	Who is the most *aggressive* communicator in your family? Why?	You want to use the phone, but your sister has been on it for the past two hours. Give two responses—one *aggressive* and one *assertive*.	Name one communication strength and one communication weakness you have as an entire family.
Family Time	Name two values that you have learned from your family.	If you and your family were stranded on an island, what would you suggest the family do for entertainment?	Share three things about your family for which you are thankful.

What's Buggin' You?	What's buggin' you about a sibling (or spouse)?	Demonstrate the "Rude Bug" in an athletic situation.	Which bug reminds you of your own bad manners (on those rare occasions, of course)? Why?

My second most favorite project was the Home Cooking Project. This idea started about twenty-eight years ago when I was teaching the eighth-grade independent living class at Byrd Middle School. My colleague introduced this concept to me and thought I might carry on the tradition. She had her students cook several times at home during the semester; the items did not need to be difficult or expensive, but they did have to be evaluated and signed off by a parent. When I was grading a paper, I saw that a tossed salad had been the student's food of choice for the "Freezer" option. Of course, I inquired how that salad tasted after two weeks. She said it was fine even though I told her lettuce doesn't fare well after being frozen, but since her mom signed off on the document, I didn't push any further; I just thought to myself, *I'd love to have seen a picture of that salad.*

I have used this project for many years, and my categories have grown from ten to twenty. A few years ago, I added the Culinary Experience component, which does *not* require any cooking. When I first assign this project, I usually get a lot of pushback about money or time. My response was "Are you going to eat ten times from now to the end of the semester?" Of course, the answer is "yes," and that is how I explain that this project can be as expensive or as inexpensive as they'd like as long as it meets the criteria. I also have a backup plan for any students who may be on a free or reduced lunch plan or if the family is facing hardship, etc. No doubt this project can be stressful because it requires various self-management skills. Of course, there will always be students who procrastinate until the last minute and then complain about how much money they had to spend and how they had no time to do the cooking. However, that was their choice.

In the years that I have assigned this project, there is one story I will never forget. I had a senior who was not doing so well, and I told him this project could make or break his chance of passing, but still he put it off. Finally, I reminded him it was due in four days. He told me he was going to cook with his grandmother over the weekend. I was skeptical, but I didn't say anything; I just wondered what was going to happen. Well, he and his grandmother did all the cooking in one weekend—they cooked seven items, answered all the questions, took three photos of each dish, printed everything in color, and organized it in a notebook, just as I had explained. When he brought it to class, he proudly announced, "That is the best project I have done in high school." I was floored when he said how great the project was. What touched me even more than his comment were the comments I read from both he and his grandmother. Her responses touched me so much that I cried while I read on. She said this project provided an invaluable experience for both of them. His comments were similar, except he added, "When she's gone, I will always have this memory." I should have worn waterproof mascara!

Below are the options I give the students. It is really a fun project to hear about and definitely to read about. Bon appétit!

Cooking Options			
1. Blast from the Past	6. Freeze It!	11. Nailed It	16. Small Appliance
2. Cooking w/ Grandma	7. Garnishes Galore	12. New Recipe	17. Snacktivities
3. Copy Cat	8. International Ingredients	13. Nifty Names	18. Special Diets
4. Family Tradition	9. K-9 Cui$ine	14. Recipe Math	19. Traditional Twist
5. Feeding a Friend	10. Mad for Meringue	15. Short Cut	20. Working w/ Yeast

Culinary Experiences		
21. Campfire Cooking	24. Dinner Table 2020	27. The Ultimate Comfort Food
22. Christmas Cuisine	25. Helping Hands	28. Unique Eats
23. Dining In	26. Restaurant Critique	29. Vacation Vittles

My third favorite project was the result of a new performance-based assessment model our district was implementing called GRASPS. The model requires the student to take on a role for a specific scenario and then create their project product as they work through the details. *My First Kitchen* was the project I created for my Foods II class. Before assigning the project, I explained, discussed, and showed students things they would need to consider in order to organize a kitchen in a logical, efficient manner. I especially pointed out that the upper cabinets are quite a bit more narrow, so they would need to pay attention when "storing" the items.

I used my own kitchen layout for this project and had a CAD student create the floor plan with numbered storage areas to make the organizational component more efficient and effective. I also chose my kitchen so I could give the students details regarding sizes of cabinets, locations to consider, etc. Once I finished going over all the basic information, I explained the project, GRASPS style.

- **G**oal—Stock and organize your first kitchen
- **R**ole—Recent college graduate; first time tenant
- **A**udience—Ms. Humphreys/other adult/peers
- **S**ituation—You have recently graduated from college and are renting your first apartment. Your first task is to set up your new kitchen with appropriate tools, equipment, dinnerware, etc.; however, you are *not* buying any food items, but you will indicate where you would store them on your floor plan. Your apartment is equipped with the following major appliances: stove, refrigerator, dishwasher, and microwave.

    For graduation gifts, you received gift cards from the following stores: Target gift cards $300 total; Walmart cards $150 total; Bed, Bath & Beyond cards $225 total; and from Home Goods or Ikea for $125. You must spend each "card" down to about two or three dollars. Included in your purchases must be three small kitchen appliances, one of which needs to be multipurpose (e.g., food processor, toaster oven, etc.). In order to get the most for your money,

use consumer skills to comparison shop for at *least one* of your small kitchen appliances. Once you purchase all your items, you will need to organize your kitchen in an efficient and logical manner.
- **Product**—Select a format to organize and submit your work. For example, Google Slides, Google Docs, trifold board, etc.

Critical Thinking Skills
- Use the given floor plans to "organize" your kitchen; complete the numbered storage chart.
- Provide a written rationale to support your storage choices.

Consumer Skills
- Create itemized receipts to show how you "spent" your money; don't forget to include sales tax.
- Each receipt must show the *tax* at the bottom just like a real receipt; do *not* include tax on each item.
- Comparison shop for at least one small kitchen appliance.

Peer/Adult Critique
- Share your finished project with one other student and one adult; ask them to critique your work using the TAG criteria (**T**ell something you like, **a**sk a question, and **g**ive a suggestion).
- Using one of the following recipes—pasghetti pizza', barbecue cups, chocolate Krispie cookies, chicken casserole, lasagna, pasta a la carbonara—evaluate another student's kitchen for efficiency.

ELA Skills
- See "Project Summary" page.

Standards
- FCS content standard: 1.1 Analyze strategies to manage multiple roles and responsibilities.

- FCS content standard: 1.2 Demonstrate transferable and employability skills in school, community, and workplace settings.
- FCS content standard: 2.1 Demonstrate management of individual and family resources such as food, clothing, shelter, health care, recreation, transportation, time, and human capital.
- FCS content standard: 2.1.5 Apply consumer skills to decisions about housing, utilities, and furnishings.

This project forces students to make many decisions as it is very subjective. I have students who love having the freedom to make all their own decisions, and I have ones who hate it. This type of assignment is designed so students can take ownership of their learning. Regardless of how the project is presented, there are always answers or information that just makes me shake my head and go "What the heck?" My favorite examples are usually from the comparison shopping component, but I get giggles from other ones too. The requirement was to comparison-shop for *one* multipurpose *appliance*, meaning it had a plug. It also means they had to use the stores associated with their "gift cards." Without fail, I get responses like this:

- The student who did the comparison shopping for a coffee mug! *Seriously?*
- The student who did the comparison between a blender, a mixer, and a set of measuring spoons instead of the same product from three stores. *Oh my!*
- The student who picked stores that weren't on the list but "bought" it with a Walmart gift card. *I really can't win.*
- The student who did comparison shopping for a potholder. *I kid you not!*
- One of my favorites was the student who made all his receipts with only whole numbers. "Why don't your items have any numbers after the decimal?" His response was, "It was easier to add that way." *OMG!*

- After looking at the kitchen floor plans I asked, "Why is the electric skillet in the cabinet above the microwave?" "Because it's not used too often." "That is a good point. However, I think you forgot there is a ventilation pipe smack dab in the middle of the cabinet." *Rolling my eyes.*
- The student who bought a set of pots and pans with a rack that could be wall-mounted; however, it was "mounted" on a wall that didn't exist! I spoke to her individually and explained that a half-wall means the upper half is "missing." *Oy vey.*
- The student who put the trash can on the counter. "Why is the trash can on the counter?" I asked. "You said we could keep things there that we use often." I didn't know if I should have laughed or cried because he actually listened to what I said, but the point clearly didn't get through.
- After looking at some receipts, I asked, "Where is the tax?" "I didn't do it because I didn't have enough money on the card." "Guess what? You will need to recalculate all your receipts." "Should I get you an abacus?" "What's that?" "One of the very first tools to calculate tax!"
- "Why is there a comforter set on your receipt?" "You said we could buy other things." "Yes, anything to do with the kitchen, like plates, flatware, etc."
- "Why is there a stand mixer in the drawer intended for dishcloths, etc.?" "That is where my mom keeps hers." "How does she get something that big into such a small space?" "She pulls the drawer out and the mixer pops up." "Who installed your kitchen, a magician?"

Of course, there are also the students who "get it." They do an amazing job, and I can tell who has spent time in their kitchen at home. What I find odd is that the majority of students have a difficult time creating a list of items for their kitchen even though they can look in the lab areas or at home, etc. To help them over this obstacle, I have them create equipment lists for four recipes that we made in Foods I. I explain that most likely what they have on their lists will be a good starting place.

CHAPTER 10

Hired or Fired?

IN 1975, MY PARENTS BOUGHT SPRINGER'S HOMEMADE Ice Cream in Stone Harbor, New Jersey. It had been my father's dream to own this business one day because it is a place where his grandfather had taken him when he was a "youngster." It was through this experience that I learned the importance of having a strong work ethic.

I began working at our store at the age of eleven, and for over forty years, I spent my summers working the business and spending time with my family. When working with a family business, you see all the moving parts required to make a business successful. Even though I was only eleven, I learned how to scoop ice cream, in spite of being too short to reach all the flavors, learned how to communicate with customers, and most importantly, I learned the importance of showing up on time and being ready to work. Many times my sister and I "pulled" double shifts because an employee called out or was a "no-show." That is a disadvantage of being part of a family business, but the benefits usually outweigh the disadvantages.

Over the years, my mom used different time card systems, and when she was no longer using the "ancient" one, I asked if I could have it for my classroom. She wondered why, and I said, "I am not sure, but as a teacher, you never know what tools may come in handy."

In 1994, my seventh-grade teen living class was getting ready to embark on a journey they never saw coming. I wanted to teach the career development unit differently this particular time, so I created *Teen Living Inc*. I wanted to provide an authentic experience at their learning level, so each student was "employed" by me and was "paid" minimum wage. To demonstrate employability skills, the employees were responsible for clocking in, clocking out, and working in a responsible manner during class time. As they were honing their skills, they worked on a company project, a career bifold board.

The students seemed excited about this idea until I told them they had to clock out whenever they left class for the bathroom, locker, water fountain, etc. Without fail, there was pushback, but I was ready. I had my guns loaded, so to speak. They tried to convince me that was unfair because at a real job, you don't do that. Of course, I agreed, but then I had them do the math with me. If an employee works an eight-hour day and takes a fifteen-minute break, they would still be working approximately 97 percent of the time. If the students took a fifteen-minute break out of our ninety-minute block class, that means they are only working 83 percent of their day…not great news for the boss. That seemed to clear things up, and I made my point.

How do I teach the students the importance of "calling out" in a professional manner? Since this was long before each student had a school email, I explained that if they were absent, they had to write a simple note with the date and explanation for the absence. If they did this, they would not be paid, but they would avoid a "ding" on their evaluation because they showed responsibility. If a person did not give me the note, I explained that was similar to not showing up for work without telling your boss, which is a big no-no. They were also required to use time wisely, put forth their best effort, and put the resources back in the correct place—not as easy as it sounds.

What I did not tell them in advance was about "Employee Appreciation Day." I explained that most workplaces do some sort of appreciation event because without employees, the company cannot be successful. Our Employee Appreciation Day consisted of my making homemade Oreo ice cream in my fancy ice cream machine, which

I also inherited from the family business, and a few other snack type foods while we pretended it was a "paid" holiday. They were psyched about food and getting paid to have fun—they were seventh graders, so it did not take much to make them happy.

At the end of the project, the employees received an employee evaluation based on their work performance. I talked to the students individually about what they liked and what they disliked about *Teen Living Inc.* as well as their own strengths and weaknesses. The one-to-one experience gave them a taste of how an interview works. It was at this point that I determined if they were hired or fired. I used a large stamp—Hired or Fired—to put on their employee folders, which they were allowed to keep. In addition to the evaluation, the employees were "paid" with a *Teen Living Inc.* paycheck. The paycheck allowed the students to see the hours worked and, of course, Uncle Sam's portion. It was my hope that by giving the students an opportunity to "work" they would have a better understanding of a real job. The unit went really smoothly, and I used this idea many times throughout my career. I didn't have to Fire anyone until years later.

At Three Fires Middle School in Michigan, I was teaching a sixth-grade creative living class which was very similar to the teen living class I taught in Virginia. In this particular class, I had a student named Alex. Alex was advanced for his age, and the entire time I was explaining the *Teen Living Inc.* concept, he said nothing but was very intent with his expressions. This class had split lunch, so we had the first twenty-five minutes of class, then lunch, and then returned for the remainder. I instructed the students that they did not need to clock out to leave for lunch because they all left at the same time, but they did have to clock back in. Alex was one of the first students back from lunch that day, and with a very serious look on his face, he said, "You know, if you buy us hovercrafts, we could get back faster which means we can work more."

I said, "We don't have the money for that."

And without skipping a beat, he said, "Well, who is the CFO, you know the chief financial officer?"

Immediately, I said, "I am, and we still don't have the money."

He continued with, "Well, can I be the CEO?"

I said, "I do that too."

He continued with, "How about the COO?"

That one stumped me for a brief second, and since I didn't answer him fast enough, he explained, "Chief operations officer."

I replied, 'That's my job as well."

After that, he was content and went to his seat as I explained the "product" they would be making as my "employee." It was a needlepoint plastic canvas coaster designed to help them with the employability skills—following directions, paying attention to detail, and following rules. Working with needles, yarn, and shears helped to improve their eye-hand coordination as well as to help improve dexterity and how to use resources properly, etc. After the coaster was finished, they moved on to make a tissue box cover, which used the same skills, so they had a good foundation to work on their own. The group I had at the time was a handful; at least that is what I was told. There was one student in particular who drove a lot of other teachers crazy, and when they heard that I was giving him a needle and shears, they were a bit taken back. I told them that he was one of my best students and I think that is because his hands were busy the entire time and gave him no "downtime." Because he caught on pretty quickly, others went to him for help if there was a long line waiting for my help. I never had a problem with him.

An unexpected benefit to having their hands busy and working in a laid-back environment was their ability to chat with students they would not have done before—and the use of Tech Decks was nonexistent. If you've never had the experience of trying to teach while little skateboards are flipped over and over, you must be a brand-new teacher!

This is another Alex story. As the students were coming back from lunch one day, one little guy was saying "I'm a Casanova, I'm a Casanova" as he skipped to his seat.

Well, Alex stood up, put his hands on his hips (like a mother does), and sternly asked, "Do you know what a Casanova is?"

"No," said the student with a quiet and hesitant tone.

"That is a man who woos women!"

I don't know if the student knew what Alex meant, but he took his seat and didn't peep for the rest of the class. Alex is one of those unforgettable students. When I called and told my mom that story, she cracked up, and then without getting off the phone, she told my dad, and he said, something like, "Way to go, little guy."

A few years ago, I was teaching a career exploration class. It was the last block of the day, and the students were mostly ninth and tenth grade. After weeks of struggling with many different classroom management challenges, I announced that they would be getting a new seating chart on Monday and that they were allowed to pick one person to sit beside. In order for me to create the seating chart, each student was required to send me an email indicating that they spoke to their potential partner so I knew they were both in agreement with the arrangement. If I did not receive the email on time, they sat wherever I put them.

This new chart worked for a bit, but then I was back to pulling out my hair, or in my case pulling it "off," and decided it was time for the time clock. The following Monday, I explained the expectations and rules for time clock use. I made sure to explain that falsifying a time card, regardless of how it was done, was an automatic "termination." The student who was the most trying asked if he could get fired so he didn't have to do the work.

I said, "Sure, but then you'd have to do a research paper instead of the work we will be doing."

He opted to stay, but eventually he was fired for various reasons. High school students didn't buy into the concept too much, but the time-clock concept worked great, and the distractions, goofing off, etc. toned down as well; however, the minute the project was done, they were back to their old ways. Luckily, the semester was almost over.

CHAPTER 11

My Hat Collection

TEACHING HAS NEVER BEEN A JOB TO me—it's been a career with a lot of adventure and a lot of "hats." I challenged myself in ways I never thought possible, and I continue to do so. When I was an assistant basketball coach, my family was a bit shocked because I have never been a sports fan; but when I began coaching soccer, Mom said, "Who are you and what have you done with my daughter?"

My mom always referred to me as a late bloomer just like my grandmother Humphreys. I didn't care for that phrase because I felt as if I was doing something wrong or taking too long to get myself on the right track. I now realize that being a late bloomer is not a bad thing because all the experiences I had prior to becoming a teacher have only made me a better teacher. Besides, my students are very wide-eyed when I tell them that I was put on academic probation at one point and fired from a job in my early twenties. I tell them it took me a while to become a teacher, but I have no regrets about how I "got here." Turning failures into learning opportunities is not always an easy thing to do, so I try to model my philosophy to students, players, etc.

When I announced to my soccer team that I would not be returning as their soccer coach, the girls asked why, and I said I wanted to wear a different hat for a bit. I was changing roles and taking on more responsibilities, such as department chair, EFE coordinator, yearbook sponsor, and the school newspaper editor.

In 1999, I was offered the position of the Education for Employment (EFE) coordinator for Byrd Middle School. EFE was a CTE class for students who were considered at risk on several levels. At the time, the students enrolled in this class could not have an IEP or a 504 plan as those students already had support in place. My students were at risk in other ways. The purpose of the class was to help them learn and demonstrate employability skills so they could move to high school with a better foundation. During the first nine weeks, I worked with the students in the classroom to develop and demonstrate workplace skills. Once they learned how to write a résumé, a cover letter, and complete some interviewing skills, they were placed with one of our teachers as a teacher's aide and were paid the minimum wage. This was long before students were not allowed to work as teacher aides due to privacy issues. My students were required to keep a "work" journal so I could read and ask questions about their experiences. The work journal also allowed students to practice legible handwriting and proper grammar. Another requirement was to keep accurate time cards to ensure they were paid correctly. When they received their first paycheck, the first thing I heard was something like "What the heck? That's not much money." Once they all quieted down, we discussed the deductions and the difference between gross and net pay. One of the biggest challenges I faced was that some of these students didn't have faith in themselves because school had not been easy for them in various ways.

The dynamics of the class were varied, and it was my job to get them to work as a team and to support each other through the highs and lows. Of course, there was always at least one student who seemed to be the "problem" or the "bad" apple. I struggled for a bit and then acted on an idea that I thought would be the glue to hold everyone together as a team instead of individuals. The principal, Harry Simmons, loved the idea, and with his approval, I took my students to a challenge course in Doswell, Virginia. Throughout the day, the students were faced with various challenges that required the ultimate level of team work if they were to succeed. Basically, it was a "ropes" course designed to be a team-building experience, and the students connected that day and became supportive of each other throughout the remainder of the course.

One of the first things I did to change the look and feel of the EFE class was to mandate appropriate working attire. I ordered embroidered polo shirts with the school and program name and required them to wear khaki pants or something similar, but jeans were not allowed. If they didn't dress appropriately, they did not work for the day. I required a dress code for a couple of reasons. One reason was so the staff could quickly identify one of my students, and if they saw something that was inappropriate, I was informed. On the flip side, I was also informed of positive "good citizen" type actions. The other reason for the uniform was to provide a sense of belonging, which many of them did not have. At the time, I think my district required at least a 2.5 GPA in order to participate in sports, and some of my students did not meet that criteria, at least when I first met them. Because of the positive changes I made to the EFE program I won the Teacher of the Year award. I was honored and surprised to receive a brass engraved apple, which I still proudly display.

My second year EFE experience was quite different from my first year. This was what I wrote in the front of the Little Kitchen cookbook.

> *The story...*
>
> *Once upon a time, there was a teacher, me, who had the glorious opportunity to teach a curriculum called "Education for Employment" (EFE). This was my second year with the program, and so I was looking forward to working with my new group of students. Thank goodness, things don't always turn out as planned.*
>
> *This particular group of students presented quite a challenge for me. Everything that had been successful before was a definite bomb! The students were frustrated with me, and I was frustrated*

because I couldn't find the "connection" I had managed to find the year before.

As the first semester progressed, both students and teacher became more stressed. I had to think of a solution before it was too late!

With a little creativity and my background in the food industry, I presented our principal, Dr. Jepson, with a plan—the Little Kitchen.

Everyone loves restaurants, but teachers don't have the opportunity to frequent them during the school day, so the plan was to bring the restaurant to the teachers.

The EFE students prepared and served the first "Little Kitchen" on February 15, 2001, and the "connection" was made. From that day forward, my EFE students and I have gotten along famously—well, most days anyway.

I am grateful that I found myself challenged with this group of students because if things had gone as planned, there would not have been a "Little Kitchen."

We have created a cookbook so that you may continue to enjoy the "Little Kitchen" delights. I hope you will remember the fun times we had this year during this new adventure. We thank you for your patronage and look forward to seeing you next year as the "Little Kitchen" strikes again.

Ms. Gloria C. Humphreys

Sadly, the following year, we didn't have enough students to run a section of EFE. I was disappointed but was grateful for the two years I did have the program. The following year, my FCCLA students continued the "Little Kitchen" tradition.

In 1999, I became the yearbook advisor, and the first book I sponsored was published in 2000 entitled "The Opening Act" because we were entering a new era. The theme of the book aligned with various theater references. Our table of contents was:

> Spotlight on Byrd: An Introduction
> Cast of Characters: Student Life
> Stars of the Show: Grade-Level Student Pictures
> Directors and Producers: Directors (administration), Producers (teaching staff)
> Behind the Scenes: Clubs and Organizations
> Lights, Camera, Action: Sports

In 2001, our book theme was "Quest…Exploring, Discovering, Being." When I saw the book cover in Jostens catalog, I knew I wanted to use it, so I thought up an idea, and the kids took it from there. Middle school is like a voyage or quest in that each grade level pushes students to discover themselves and hone in on individuality. Everyone knows middle school is a problem, a joy, a headache, every parents' nightmare, etc. However, everyone needs to make the best of their voyage because they only get one chance as they move toward becoming a teen instead of being a "tween."

The way I explained my idea was that sixth graders are "exploring" this new world called middle school. The seventh graders are "discovering" more and more about their voyage, and the eighth graders are just "being" who they are in this soon-to-end voyage. This particular book was very special to us because it won an award from Jostens for creativity and originality and something else that I can't remember. It remains one of my favorite books, and that was twenty years ago.

The table of contents was:

> The Voyage: Introduction and Explanation of the Theme
> Exploring, Discovering, Being: Student Life
> Being Me: Grade-Level Student Pictures
> The Navigators: Administrator, Teachers, and Other Staff

Being Involved: Clubs and Organizations
Discovering Limits: Sports

In case people don't know how yearbook publishing works, the theme is usually determined in the spring, so when fall comes, everyone is ready to get started. As usual, the staff and I had another really cool theme planned and then 9/11 happened, and we had to change gears. Jostens quickly created new cover options because the entire world was upside down and yearbooks would most likely need a new look.

In the 2002 edition, our theme was going to be based on blue jeans, so luckily, one of the new covers was red, white, blue and denim, which was a perfect fit for us. The "Time 2 be US" theme still allowed the students to work on some of the ideas they talked about in the spring. This book was much harder to produce for us for many reasons; however, the kids pulled it off and were very proud of their accomplishment. The table of contents showcased their concept of time.

>What Time Is It? Introduction
>Time 2 Be Us: Student Life
>Sixth-Grade: Time 2 Ask Questions
>Seventh-Grade: Second Time Around
>Eighth-Grade: Last Time Around
>Double Time: Focus on Twins
>Time 2 Smile: Grade-Level Pictures
>Time 2 Behave: Administration
>Time 2 Learn: Faculty
>Time 2 Lead, Join, and Perform: Clubs and Organizations
>Game Time! Sports
>Time 2 Move On: Closing, Poetry Winner, World Beat

The 2003 yearbook cover had us stumped because we knew we wanted to "go" back thirty years and do a "Then and Now" concept, but none of the cover options fit our idea, so we splurged and used one of the graphic artists from Jostens. We loved the design, but we couldn't agree on a color theme. One day, while I was doing laundry for one of my food classes, I looked at the detergent bottle and really liked the colors they used—yellow, purple, and green—and so did the students; the rest is history.

The table of contents was:

    Now and Then: Intro
    Here and There: Student Life
    Me and You: Grade-Level Pictures
    On and Off Stage: Performing Arts
    Before and After: Clubs and Organizations
    Winning and Losing: Sports
    Then and Now: Closing and World Beat

I did not know it at the time, but I would be moving to Michigan at the end of the school year, so that was the last yearbook I would supervise. I am very lucky to have worked with such great students in class and be part of an amazing staff.

CHAPTER 12

Moving to the Mitten

WHEN I FIRST MOVED TO MICHIGAN AND was learning my way around, I would ask various people questions about the state and what types of places I should visit. Next thing I knew, they were holding up their right hand and pointing to a specific area.

"What's with the hand?" I finally asked.

"Michigan is *The Mitten State*, and it's common to help newcomers by using their hand as a map."

Another helpful tip was using the word HOMES to remember the great lakes—Huron, Ontario, Michigan, Erie, Superior. I have never been good with directions, so combining the 'mitten' with HOMES was helpful as I settled in.

My husband (at the time) and I both liked snow but for very different reasons. I liked snow because I am a teacher, and the first snow day of the year is just awesome—no other way to say it. My husband, on the other hand, liked snow because he got to use his new shovel to clear the driveway—yes, he was excited to use a shovel, but not just any shovel. He was using his Yooper Scooper! It did a great job as I watched from the comfort of the sofa with the dog beside me and a cup of hot cocoa in hand.

Learning that a Yooper is not a shovel manufacturing company but the word used to describe the people who lived in the Upper

Peninsula added more info to my new found interest in "All Things Michigan." I enjoyed learning about the culture and how typical Midwesterners lived. We went to the Upper Peninsula once, and as we were driving through a small, Mayberry-esque town, I asked, "Why are all the STOP signs on the sidewalks? Why are they so short?"

He told me those were for the snowmobilers because that was a very popular way to travel to and from town. I added that information to my "list," and as our trip progressed, I learned that pop is the correct name for a beverage, not soda. I also learned a favorite Upper Peninsula dish is called a pasty (pass-tee). When I placed my order, I pronounced it as "pastie," and my husband started laughing. I didn't know that what I said referred to nipple coverage on exotic dancers; with my eyes wide, I thought to myself, *We're not in Mayberry anymore!*

My husband and I both loved log cabins and fireplaces, so when I found a log cabin hotel with a fireplace and an in-room jacuzzi, I booked a room for two nights. It was sort of our honeymoon because moving, getting a job, etc. had been time-consuming. What I did not know is that the Great Wolf Lodge is an indoor water park for families, so we laughed about my lack of ability to book romantic destinations; I should have looked closer at the brochure. Oh, well. The next time we visited Great Wolf Lodge was when my parents, my sister, and my four-year-old nephew joined us. You definitely fit in when you are toting around a small human, but two adults on a honeymoon is a bit awkward. A few months later, I redeemed myself by renting a log cabin in Grayling, Michigan, where we spent Thanksgiving. We were the first people to rent this cabin, and so we wrote a note in the cabin "journal" that we loved our stay and would surely be back again. We did go back a year or two later, and it was fun to read about all the people that had visited, and it was fun to read the entry we wrote.

Early on in my Michigan Education 101, I learned that I was pronouncing and/or spelling things incorrectly, and as a teacher, misspelling and mispronunciation drove me nuts; however, I was a victim of my own pet peeve. I come from Virginia where Charlottesville is home to the University of Virginia and pronounced "Char-lit," but in Michigan, Charlotte is pronounced Shar-LOT. Then there is Mackinac Island which I pronounced as Mack-in-ack, but it's really pronounced MACK-in-awe. One of my worst flubs was Sault St. Marie (Sue Saint Marie), which I pronounced Salt St. Marie. I was not even close. Luckily, I learned the correct pronunciation before I saw one of my students wearing a Sault St. Marie sweatshirt, and I impressed her when I pronounced it correctly. There were many other names I flubbed on, but I was still learning. I am certain that if I were to visit more places north of Lansing, I would make plenty of mistakes. I have lived in Michigan for over twenty years, and I am still making mistakes, but not as many. You can take the teacher out of the classroom, but you can't take the classroom out of the teacher. That is just how we're wired.

A few other things I learned about Michigan was how to dodge potholes, how to master the Michigan left, and how to waddle like a penguin. If you have not had the opportunity to drive the Ohio Turnpike, you are missing some of the smoothest roads and best rest areas ever made; however, the transition from Ohio roads to Michigan roads was as sad and quick as Cinderella's carriage turning back into a pumpkin. I hit my first pothole not long after I reached US Route 23 and thought I had damaged my undercarriage for sure, but luckily, I did not. I have heard many Michiganders say that dodging potholes in Michigan is considered an Olympic sport, to which I agree 100 percent!

When my mom visited for the first time, she almost had a heart attack while I was turning left on a red light. I had to explain that the Michigan left is safer than trying to make left hand turns at a busy intersection. She still didn't like it, but then I reminded her that she never had a problem navigating the Jersey jughandle. Personally, I'd take a Michigan left any day over a Jersey jughandle.

My first encounter with black ice was in the parking lot of Jackson High School. I was wearing my Dansko clogs and walking gingerly toward the door when I was distracted by a bumper sticker that read, "A House Divided." I didn't know what that meant, so I wanted to take a closer look. As I turned my body ever so slightly, I slipped and landed on my backside. All the "cushioning" in the world was not going to break that fall, and I had not yet heard of the "winter waddle."

A few years ago, I read about how many Michiganders and other winter walkers may find that walking like a penguin can be key to avoiding slips/falls on ice and snow. Let's face it, penguins are the masters of balance when it comes to walking on ice, so maybe we should take a page from their playbook. I doubt I'll ever look as cute as a penguin when I practice my winter waddle, but here's how it's done: Keep your center of gravity over your feet as much as possible; walk flat-footed; take shorter, shuffle-like steps; and keep your arms at your sides, not in your pockets. This information may have been helpful that day in the parking lot, but let's face it, clogs are not a good choice for snow or ice no matter what. Since that day, I have also learned that a house divided is when home team loyalties are divided between University of Michigan and Michigan State University.

CHAPTER 13

I Must Have Been Absent That Day

I MUST HAVE BEEN ABSENT THE DAY my professor discussed how easy classroom management was going to be because I was *clueless* for years. No one can teach you what it takes to keep your own classroom under control, so figuring out that balance can be very tricky. During my second year of teaching, my classroom management skills were considered unsatisfactory, and so I was put on a strict management plan. I had to meet with my administrator weekly so we could discuss my progress. The following is from my personal journal.

January 27, 1995

I know I am a poor disciplinarian, and it definitely showed on Wednesday when Mrs. Diggs came in to observe. It was the most chaotic class of the semester! I had made Sand (the vanilla version of dirt cake) for the class because I felt bad that we hadn't cooked more. There I was trying to serve a snack to a class that was totally out of control! I was also trying to help a few stragglers that hadn't finished their sewing project. The behavior was horrible, and I just let it happen. Then I realized several

> students had taken almost all the gummy worms. There I was completely embarrassed and humiliated. I know Mrs. Diggs was not pleased with what she saw because she came back the next day, but things were still rough. When a class sews, it creates an environment that appears to be completely unorganized. Sometimes it actually is unorganized, other times it is just organized chaos.

February 11, 1995

> I have been so busy this week I haven't had a chance to catch up on what's happening. School has been going pretty well despite the lousy observation I had a few weeks ago. Thank goodness Mrs. Diggs did come to a class for an observation that was just wonderful. It was during second period, and it was smooth as silk! I was so glad she popped in that day. Overall, my evaluation for the year was great—I was very pleased. I will be anxious to see how it compares to the one from last year.

Things were rough for quite a while, but I decided that the students were more important than following a strict lesson plan, so I decided to work on getting to know the students instead of riding shotgun over them. The sixth-grade students were an easy sell because they just wanted to have fun and were grateful they weren't in elementary school anymore. From my personal journal, I found this quote: *I really like the middle schoolers. I know I hated them in the beginning, but I really learned to like them. Once I figured out how to deal with their "activity" level, things became a lot easier.* At one point, I had my sixth graders believing I could not graduate college until I passed the "teacher raised eyebrow stare." Of course, in the end, I came clean, and they said I owed them some candy for "telling a fib."

In 2015, our district (Howell Public Schools) provided the training for Capturing Kids Hearts (CKH), a program developed by Flip Flippen. On the front cover of the participant manual is this quote from Flip Flippen, "If you have a child's heart...You have his head." At the core of this training is one word—relationships. If we teachers can't build relationships with our students, then teaching them can be extremely difficult. I thought I was doing a great job with my classes, but after taking the training, the connection with the students skyrocketed while the classroom distractions plummeted. To this day, I spend the first several days doing a variety of activities I learned from that program. Two of my favorite activities, *Warp Speed* and *Clump*, remain classroom favorites.

Another thing I must have been absent from was the discussion of how to prepare for the death of a student. One Sunday evening, I returned home to a voicemail message from my principal. He needed me to call him as soon as possible, but it was too late to call, so I had to wait until the next day. Needless to say, I didn't sleep that night. When I pulled into the school parking lot the next morning, I knew something was not right. I went to the office, and that was where I learned that one of my students had committed suicide by shotgun and was found by his younger brother. I was devastated, and I am not one who can hold back tears very well, so I didn't even try. His guidance counselor followed his schedule for the day so that students could get help if needed. I just recalled seeing his seat, and then it was as if a brick struck my chest and knocked the wind out of me. Immediately, I thought to myself, *Did I miss something? Could I have done anything differently?* But as many of us know through experience, that is a very typical reaction. This was the first funeral I attended, and it was gut-wrenching. Unfortunately, that would not be the last funeral I attended.

At Three Fires Middle School, I taught eighth grade health, and one of the units was about death and dying. My colleague, Debbie Miller, had been teaching the curriculum for years, and each year, she organized a field trip to a local funeral home for our students. I thought this idea was insane, and so I asked her why. She told me that during her first year of teaching, a colleague had died very unexpectedly, and she was nervous about going to the funeral home because she had never been to one before.

She explained that she organized the trip so the students would have a better understanding of the funeral process with the hopes that when they did have to go to one, they would not feel as uncomfortable as she did. Prior to the field trip, we discussed our expectations, which included respectful dress attire and that jeans were not permitted. During the field trip, the students were able to visit the embalming room, the casket room, and the viewing room. The funeral director explained the importance of the viewing and the funeral process because they help families find some peace and closure. The students thought it was a bit odd and morbid, but a few years later, a fellow student died suddenly, and they told Mrs. Miller how grateful they were for the funeral field trip.

CHAPTER 14

The Grocery Getter

NOT LONG AFTER I ARRIVED IN MICHIGAN, I found a teaching position at Jackson High School. My two years at JHS were quite eye-opening on many levels, and I believe the students taught me more than I taught them. Since I had come from a very affluent school district, I was pretty ignorant when it came to working with students of poverty. My journal entry says it all.

August 27, 2004

I just spent two days in an awesome staff development. The SEA got two speakers from "aha! Process Inc." who spoke about poverty. It was very rewarding and eye-opening. So many of the things we discussed were applicable, and it made me feel better knowing that I already did a lot of the techniques but had put them aside last year because I thought it wouldn't work. For example, I used to put pictures on my vocabulary to help the kids remember it. Well, that is one of the things that is recommended.

> *I wish we had more time to discuss discipline, but I guess I'll have to do that on my own. Mrs. Ellis did say that children of poverty need more structure in the classroom. Because they live in the present and the instinct is to survive, they need to know what's expected now. So much of what (and) how they live is governed by the survival mode.*

I wish I had this information during my first year at Jackson, but as the saying goes, better late than never.

One day, I was talking to another faculty member about the attendance issues and how frustrated I was with the situation. The attendance inconsistencies made it difficult to provide make-up work, food labs, etc. I could not require the student to cook the recipe at home, so I was constantly trying to find ways to accommodate their needs while holding them accountable. She listened and then told me some stories about her own students. Over the years, she had several students who were known to miss school multiple times and for various reasons. Some of those students had to stay home to take care of a sick sibling or babysit for younger siblings because the parents could not afford to take time off from work. In other cases, the student had to stay home so the repairman could come fix the heater. I was stunned when I heard this because "I never saw that coming." I felt horrible for complaining about attendance when the students were not in a great situation to be successful according to my standards.

The next time I taught Maslow's hierarchy of needs, I recalled these stories and realized pretty quickly that many students were living at the bottom level of the pyramid. I suppose I had always taken basic needs for granted and just assumed my audience had the same perspective and experience as I had. When I realized how many of my students were struggling with the most basic needs, I was at a loss for how to help. At first, I felt inadequate, and as I learned more about the culture of my students, I realized I had some serious learning to do and bridges to build. I tried to learn about each student through observation because as an introvert, I "see much but say little." This angle needed to change if I really wanted to get to know the students, so I began answering their questions as honestly as I could. My students were not shy about asking about my personal life.

One day, a student just asked, "You got you some kids?"

I said, "No."

"Why not?" she asked.

"Because I must have left them off the grocery list…bread, milk, eggs, and kids. Just because many students can get pregnant does not mean that's easy for everyone."

From another student, I was asked "What kind of car you drive?"

"A Subaru Outback…a station wagon."

Someone else yelled out, "That's a grocery getter, and I bet you gonna get you some kids too!"

My car has been called the grocery getter ever since.

*****

Jackson was located right across the street from a maternity home for pregnant teens, and several of my students were pregnant which had its own set of challenges for me. Speaking of children, I taught a child development class which was something I had never taught before. In this class, we read three books based on the Hamilton High books by Marilyn Reynolds: *Too Soon for Jeff*, *Detour for Emmy*, and *Baby Help*. These books were a very popular part of the class, especially when I read aloud. I had no idea that reading aloud would be such a popular activity, but I really enjoyed the experience. Reading about teen pregnancy from both the female and male points of view made for excellent class discussions, especially for me because I would have never had this experience in any of the schools I had taught at before. However, their favorite book was *Baby Help*; it's a story about a teen mother who is juggling school, work, raising a baby, and living with her abusive boyfriend, the baby's father.

The books were perfect for my students because they were relatable and written for seventh grade and up.

Another story from my Jackson days is about Henry; he was quite the character. He was a junior and pretty much the entire student body knew him. One day, he had on a T-shirt with an RIP photo on the front, and without even thinking, I said, "What does that mean?" I pointed to his T-shirt.

"Rest in peace, that's my father."

I felt like a huge idiot, but I had never seen anything like that before. He explained a bit, and I said I was sorry for not "seeing" it, and he and I connected that day; however, a few days later, he came into class and said, "Yo, Ms. Humphreys, you da dawg!"

I was not pleased with that description, so I started to get upset, and the entire class jumped in and told me that meant I was "cool." Henry said something like "I'd never 'dis' you," and I thanked him. To make this situation even better, I had Henry in my child development class; he did not choose the class but was "put" there. He hated to do any writing and managed to get me into a conversation nearly every day and *almost* always on topic. I am an introvert and cannot lecture/talk all day, but Henry made it work for both of us—he talked and asked questions, and I responded. His personality was such that in spite of being the class clown, he was not disruptive.

One day, I was talking about children's books and how they are different in structure, format, and illustrations for each stage of development. We had books in class that they would read and evaluate, but I wanted to share my favorite childhood book and share a story before they began working. My favorite book is *The Country Bunny and the Golden Shoes*, which was a baby gift to me from one of my mom's best friends. Apparently, I was attracted to the pictures in books at an early age, and that was how I began to memorize books. I told them this story my mom told me.

When I was in kindergarten, I was sitting in my mom's lap reading a book to her, but she caught me looking away from the book, and so she turned the pages out of order and realized I could not read anything at all, and I was busted! She met with my teacher and told her that I was not reading but memorizing the book based on the pictures. Of course, the teacher said that's impossible until mom asked her to read it with me. I wish I had those memory skills nowadays.

Henry asked if he could read it aloud, and I said, "You sure?"

"Yep" was the response.

Not only did he read the book aloud, but he also moved around and changed his voice to suit the characters; everyone was clapping when he was done, and he took a big bow! He graduated the following year, and as the procession was walking by, he yelled to me, "I did it!" All of us were cheering but especially Henry's teachers. I can't read that book without thinking about Henry.

My favorite story from JHS is about Tiffany. I had her for a semester class, and I watched her every day with a chip on her shoulder the size of Texas. She was a very angry person and seemed to be that way most of the time. One day, I asked to see her in the hallway and prefaced my request with "You're not in trouble." She followed me, but not before she slammed her pencil down. She immediately leaned up against the wall and folded her arms across her chest, indicating that I *was* clearly going to be the problem—body language speaks volumes.

She was very surprised when I said, "You are really smart, do you know that?"

She looked at me with wrinkled brows and said, "What?"

So I repeated myself. I asked her some questions about her school experience, and from what I gathered, her tough exterior followed her through the day. I then began to tell her what I saw in her. I told her that she is punctual, does her work thoroughly, and turns it in on time. I explained those are the types of traits you will want to keep using as you graduate and find yourself in the real world. I told her that she had a lot of potential, but because her exterior was so "hard," it was not easy for others to get to know the real person. That was all I said to her, and then we went back to class.

Little by little, I saw small changes in her behavior; the chip on her shoulder stayed awhile, but she did try to interact with more people in a more positive way. Through the rest of the semester, she continued to let down her tough exterior. Then the semester was over, and I did not see her again; however, right before graduation, she came to see me and gave me a big hug and said, "You believed in me." She also said that no one had ever talked to her that way, and she thanked me. I saw her at graduation, and she held up her diploma with a huge smile on her face.

Since FCS is part of the Career and Technical Education program, we were expected to give a work ethic grade. I tried using a weekly chart the students filled in daily, but it was a lot of work, and I was still struggling with other things, so I decided to do things my way. So what did I do? I pulled out the time clock, and every time they were "out" of class, they lost minutes, which was equal to points. Before the time clock was introduced, students were leaving the classroom as though it had a revolving door. The time clock fixed the leaving-class problem but not the dress-code problems. This was the time frame when the boys wore their pants around their thighs, with a belt and their underwear on display for the whole student body to see. The belt apparently was more for show than function, so they had to hold on to them so they didn't fall off. Administration gave us zip ties for any student who had a "pants" issue. If they didn't comply, the administration handled it. However, there is always that "one" person who tries to push the envelope. "That" student really needed suspenders, but I could not require those; however, I could require a zip tie.

One day, as he was trying his best to have me back down, I said, "Fine, if you can walk down the hall without your pants falling down, I will not make you do anything. If they fall down, then you'll have to use a zip tie."

I made sure he was okay with the idea that his pants might fall down. Of course, the entire class came out to watch, and as he started to grab the waist of his pants to hold them up, I said, "No hands allowed."

Needless to say, he then put the zip tie on, and I made my point. Moving forward, his pants stayed up at least in my class.

CHAPTER 15

Sex Ed…You Just Had to Be There!

IN 2005, I WAS HIRED AS A long-term sub at Three Fires Middle School where I met Debbie Miller, the other FCS teacher. She told me I would be teaching sixth, seventh, and eighth grade classes, which was fine with me because I had a lot of experience with middle school students. Then I was informed that the seventh-grade class was actually a health class focusing on reproductive health. I remember my eyes getting really large, but I could show no fear because I wanted the job. Little did I know that teaching this subject would be so enlightening.

I had never taught sex ed or had I taken any of the classes when I was in high school, so I was feeling a bit nervous. One icebreaker activity we did with the students is called "Male, Female, Both," an activity designed by Su Nottingham. This is not about gender identity, but it is about knowing the "right parts" for the "right system." Students have a set of cards with the various reproductive organs, and they have to put the card in the correct system. For example, the "skin" is supposed to go into the "Both" column, and then I say the "brain" goes into the female column, which usually provides a bit of laughter to make the situation less scary.

As the students were working, I was walking around to see how things were going. One student asked me, "What is this word?" He was holding an "areola" card.

I had no idea, and it took me by surprise, but the "show no fear" kicked in, and I said, "Why don't you try the process of elimination? That may help."

I wanted to jump the tables and run right into Debbie's room, but I maintained composure and went through the small office that connects our rooms. I stuck my head into her room and said, "Office, *now*!"

She excused herself and headed to me. She came in worried that something was wrong and asked, "What's wrong?"

With a frustrated look on my face, I said, "What the *hell* is an areola?"

She could not contain her laughter as she told me, "It's the dark circle around the nipple."

We both laughed and then had to wipe the tears away before heading back to our classes as if nothing happened.

Whenever either of us "needed" the other immediately, we would pop in their classroom and say, "Office, *now*!" Unfortunately, I had to use the "office" for several sex ed-related questions. At the time, it was frustrating, funny, and helpful; however, I felt so stupid because I thought how can a person my age not know about all "my parts"?

Mrs. Miller and I felt the students should learn the correct vocabulary for all units but especially for this one. We knew the information may not be easy to talk about, so we did a warm-up vocabulary "match" activity. Cards were handed out that had either the term or the definition on it. The objective was to find the student who had their match by walking around and talking to each other. After a practice run, they "got" it. This activity had multiple objectives; of course, one was content and the other ones were to have them practice social skills—eyes contact, pronunciation, talking, etc. However, instead of walking around the room to find their match, as we directed, many of them stayed in one place and yelled, "Who has penis?" "Who has sex?" or "Who has testicles?" etc. As rowdy as that may seem, it was a great way to build rapport with the students and with each other. This activity is usually the beginning of funny sex ed stories, such as this next one.

In addition to knowing the correct meaning, correct pronunciation and the correct spelling were expected. As we were discussing the terms and definitions I got to Joe and I asked what term he has, he said, "Sex."

I asked him for the spelling and the definition, and he said, "My dad says that sex is spelled *fun*!"

We all cracked up, and I nearly cried from laughing so hard; it just couldn't be helped, and I am sure it was definitely a day the kids would not forget!

As soon as class was over, I went to the cafeteria because his mom worked there. I told her what happened, and her face went beet red! The next day in class, I asked Joe if he and his dad were in the doghouse. He said his mom was mad, but his dad said, "That's my boy!" We all laughed again, and I am so glad that ended well for all involved.

Oddly enough, when we did the same activity with the female vocabulary, not one student, male or female, yelled at all. I suppose the boys thought, *There's no way I am yelling "Who has vagina?" or "Who has breasts?"*

As they expanded their knowledge of the female unit, a young man said, "Man, girls are so confusing."

With a big smile on my face, I responded with, "Yep, so if you think it's confusing now, wait until you start dating."

A year or so later, I had another great story unfold. I was discussing conception and how it takes place in the fallopian tube when a little voice says, "My dad said it was in the back seat of his car."

I believe my words were, "Okay, moving along."

As soon as class was over, I had to run and tell Debbie, and we howled. My real concern was that I would be mortified if his parents came to parent/teacher conferences because I was not sure I could keep a straight face. Luckily, they did not show up.

Our seventh-grade sex ed unit was abstinence based, so we talked about it a lot. We did some activities to help the students understand that choosing abstinence happens long before you are in a "tempting" situation. A young man raised his hand to tell me, and I quote, "My church does not believe in sex."

My brain wanted me to say, *Well that's not a very fun church!* but I ended up saying, "Well, how'd you get here?"

He turned red and said, "I mean before marriage…not after."

CHAPTER 16

"Seam"ingly Funny

WHEN I BEGAN TEACHING SEX ED, I called my sister and told her that she needed to teach Neil, my nephew, the correct anatomical terminology—no more slang. Not long after she started to "educate" him, I was telling her another funny sex ed story, and Neil, who was about five, overheard me use the word flaccid.

"What's that mean?" he said.

I looked at Mary, and she gave me a look that said, "This is your specialty."

So I said, "It's when the penis is 'soft.'"

He immediately looked into his pajama bottoms and said, "Yep, it's flaccid."

Mary and I laughed so hard that I just about wet my pants, and Neil flung himself onto his bed face first as the laughter took over his whole body.

Several years later, when Neil was around seven or eight, he walked into the living room to find grandma sewing up a seam on his teddy bear. Without skipping a beat, he said, "Grandma, thanks for sewing up her vagina."

My mother almost passed out as Neil just moseyed along, having no idea what had happened. I was not there, but I believe it ended with hysterical laughter from my mom and my sister. I am not sure my mother appreciated my drive to be honest and direct when it comes to sex because she grew up in a generation that did not discuss "things like that."

As I continued teaching sex ed, she occasionally asked if I had any more "funnies," and, of course, the answer was always "Yes, I do."

Recently, Mary reminded me that I was not the only one who had funny sex ed stories. Apparently, when Neil was about nine, he asked her about a line he heard in the movie she was watching; he wanted to know what "slapping the salami" meant. She told him, "It's when someone simulates the sex act with themselves."

And he got a look of disgust on his face and said, "Any good mother would have just lied!"

CHAPTER 17

Opposites Attract

WHEN DEBBIE MILLER AND I FIRST MET, she introduced me to the True Colors personality survey. After completing the survey, I found I was most likely a "blue," and without a doubt, Debbie was an "orange." I really didn't know how this information would impact our teaching dynamic, but as we progressed through the first few weeks of our "teamship," I became keenly aware of how an orange and a blue impact each other.

One of Debbie's favorite classroom activities was doing a cooking demonstration. I, on the other hand, hated food demos. However, that did not keep me from getting roped into hers. On more than one occasion, she would pop into my room and announce, "Let's cook today!" Of course, my sixth graders cheered and said "Yay!" Little did they know I had spent a lot of time working on a new activity for them, but how could I compete with food? Eventually, I looked at her spontaneity as a positive situation because that meant she was doing the talking and I was doing crowd control—perfect situation for an extrovert and an introvert. After a few of these "pop-up" lessons, I began to think of them as my very own snow day—a welcome surprise.

One day, we planned to co-teach the sixth grade body image lesson. We talked about media influences and how teens may feel they don't meet certain standards or they compare themselves to people that are photoshopped, etc., especially for females. We asked if anyone knew why females have wider hips than males. The answer, of course, should have been because of childbirth; however, with sixth grade, you never know what you'll get. Sure enough, a student had a different take. He stood up and put his fisted hands on his hips and proudly said, "So my mom can do this!"

CHAPTER 18

S'more Hunting

MANY OF MY STUDENTS AT THREE FIRES Middle School were avid hunters, so this time, I was prepared to be more supportive and understanding of this sport. One day, I asked a female student if she had any pictures to share.

"Yes, I do," she said and got her phone, scrolled through several until she chose the one to show me.

The picture was of the dead deer hanging upside down and bleeding, but there she was with a big smile on her face. My stomach dropped to my toes, and all I could get out was, "Look at the smile… on you, not the deer."

I have not asked to see pictures anymore. From my nonhunting brain, I suppose I was expecting a Hallmark movie camping scene—people around a campfire, making S'mores, and singing "Kumbaya"…it *never* occurred to me I would be looking at the dead deer.

Another great story revolves around two seventh-grade male students who drove me nuts because they would *not* stop talking. One day, I received an email from their parents explaining that their children would be missing school for four days to go hunting. I was *delighted* to get the news, and the four days of quiet and calm were enjoyed by all.

After the boys returned to class, they went right back to talking nonstop. This time I said, "I want to understand something. You went hunting for four days and were able to stay quiet in the little fort 'thingy' for long periods of time, is that correct?"

"Yes."

"Okay, so if I wear some fake antlers, can we pretend you are hunting so you'll be quiet?"

Without skipping a beat, Caleb said, "Can I bring a gun?"

I just burst out laughing, and for some reason, from that day on, things were much better, and I survived the rest of the quarter.

CHAPTER 19

A Labor of Love or Hell's Kitchen?

WHEN THE CELEBRITY CHEF SHOWS BEGAN, a student once asked me if Gordon Ramsey could come to class, and I asked why.

He said, "Because *Hell's Kitchen* is a great show."

My response was, "Every day we have a lab, it's like hell's kitchen, so no need for us to host a celebrity."

I don't know if they were laughing from the connection or because I said "hell." Anyway, students, past and present, often complain about not having dishwashers, and my response was "You have two good hands called dishwashers. Besides, you would miss heating the water," which we had to do at one point. That usually invoked a lot of eye-rolling and "Ughs," and I don't mean the warm fuzzy ones.

Cooking labs are by far where some of my best stories were born. At Byrd Middle School, our department had two classrooms across the hall from each other which gave us three labs in each kitchen. For the most part, when either of us teachers cooked, we used both kitchens, requiring us to move back and forth between the two.

One day, I was leaving my kitchen and heading across the hall as someone yelled out, "Ms. Humphreys, we need more baking soda."

I replied, "There's more in the pantry."

As I was walking to the other kitchen, I thought to myself, *Why would they need more baking soda when they have a whole container?*

When I asked why they needed more, one student said, "There wasn't enough."

I said, "How much did you use?"

"One-fourth cup," she replied.

I believe my eyes almost popped out of the head as I said, "The recipe calls for a 1/4 teaspoon."

In a typical student response, the whole group said, "It looks fine, they'll be great."

I shook my head and said, "Only time will tell."

When the cookies were finished baking, they pulled the baking sheets out, and the cookies were so flat that the chocolate chips resembled dead flies stuck on a fly strip—not very appetizing. The students still held onto their belief that they would be fine, so I suggested they eat one. As a matter of fact, I suggested the whole class should try one, and they did. Practically in unison, I hear gagging and "Ugh" from about five people. They couldn't even swallow the bite they bit off, and because I am a team player, I tried one too. In case you have never experienced the result of too much baking soda, let me tell you it was like licking and chewing on metal. It is a taste I do not care to repeat. I am pretty sure those students will learn to read recipes more carefully. Over the years, there have been many measuring mishaps, and those who have done it realize how paying attention to detail is necessary.

In another of my journal entries (verbatim) on 12-8-1994, I found this:

> *I survived another cooking lab yesterday! Not by much, but I did survive. I am very concerned about seventh grade because I don't feel at all comfortable w/ what's going on. I have way too many things left untold. My main problem is that I leave too much to them. I assumed they would know how to make pasta. I thought they would know what a saucepan was. I almost lost it yesterday when I saw Elicia using a mixing bowl on the range to cook her soup. Kari put her pasta shells directly into the cold*

H2O. Kylie's group dumped a good part of their macaroni on the floor. We have to finish the cleanup today because we just didn't get it finished yesterday. Before next semester, I need to come up with a project that can be done while I rotate groups to cook. It would take us at most about two days per lab if I use three groups. I need to be able to give them more time than I have. There's the possibility of cooking at the end of foods and having them cook while they sew (meaning they have to wait for their day to cook); *gut feeling say "No" to that. I'll have to do some planning on that one.*

Speaking of pasta, recently one of my classes was making lasagna, and a group placed their noodles like a tic-tac-toe board…interesting. At least they used a pot to cook the noodles unlike the group that tried to cook the noodles in a saucepan. I just don't have words for some situations.

In 1999, my eighth-grade class was working on a food history project based on *Dining Through the Decades: "The American Appetite"*; it's a series published in *The Richmond Times Dispatch*. Each group researched one decade from 1900–1990 to find historical events, changes in technology, family-eating patterns, etc. While the students were doing their research in the library, I noticed several boys all huddled around one computer, so I decided to investigate. When I looked at the screen, all I saw were Playboy Bunnies, so all I said was "Try looking up rabbits instead." I don't remember why they were worried about rabbits, but I definitely know that the Playboy Bunny was not part of my criteria. Clearly we were all still trying to master the Boolean search since there was no Google.

In addition to the research, each group selected a recipe that was popular during their decade and made it. Students had to read over the recipes which were included in the information we were using before they could consider a different one. Some students were really excited about their recipes—White Castle hamburgers, Toll House

Cookies, and Flaming Baked Alaska—other groups not so much—chicken pudding and chicken soup.

"What's wrong with chicken soup?" you might be asking yourself, and in most cases, "Nothing" is the answer; however, this recipe calls for a "whole chicken, head and feet included!" Yeah, we didn't do it that way, but the recipe was interesting, nonetheless.

Chicken Soup

1 whole chicken
2 quarts water
1/2 cup rice, cooked

1. *Take the pieces of chicken not desirable for frying—skin, head, and feet—and use giblets.*
2. *Boil in 2 quarts of water until quite tender.*
3. *Skim well while boiling.*
4. *Remove meat and bones and have ready 1/2 cup rice boiled soft and add to the broth.*
5. *Boil 10 minutes after adding rice and then strain through a wire sieve.*
6. *Add salt and pepper to taste.*

This is an excellent broth for the sick, especially one who has bowel trouble.

On lab day, the group collected their ingredients and proceeded to get to work. Things appeared to be going well, or at least I thought they did. When I walked over to see how things were going, one student said, "There's not much liquid."

I asked, "Where is the broth?"

The response was, "We drained it."

They were a bit embarrassed when I told them the "soup" comes from the juices of the chicken as it cooks in the water. I reminded them that in the 1900s, people used all the chicken because very little food went to waste.

Several years later, I had my seventh grade class at Three Fires Middle school do the same project, with the same requirements—presentation, activity, and, of course, the cooking part. This time, the group from the 1920s taught the class how to dance the Charleston as part of their presentation prior to the lab. Everyone enjoyed the show, and I thought to myself, *How many times am I going to get a group of seventh graders to dance the Charleston?* Another memory tucked away.

A few years ago, my Foods II class was working on the "Macaroni Mania" lab in preparation for a mac-and-cheese cook-off. As I was observing all the hustle and bustle, I saw one student with the powder sugar container, and I thought that was surely a twist on a pasta dish, so I went to investigate. Unfortunately, it was not a creative twist but a case of mistaken identity—they were using powdered sugar instead of flour.

When I asked why, someone said, "It was on the flour shelf."

And I said, "That may be, but it is clearly labeled powdered sugar."

Similar to previous responses, the students insisted the dish would be "fine"; my comment was, "Time will tell." I guess this situation made me realize I may have to spend more time reviewing ingredients. I guess I took some things for granted, thinking everyone knows the difference between flour and powdered sugar, but I was clearly wrong. Only one person in the group attempted to eat it, but ultimately, the food ended up in the trash.

Last spring, my students were making peach cobbler, so we could examine the functions of ingredients. According to the recipe, the butter is placed in the pan and then put into the oven to melt while the oven heats up.

A student yelled out to me, "Do we take the wrapper off?"

"Yes," I said as laughter erupted from his group.

He said, "Well, it's not listed in the directions."

I swear I can't win. If I give too many directions, someone is mad; if I don't give enough, someone else is mad. What continues to bother me is that each year, students seem to have more difficulties reading "between the lines," or in some cases, not reading at all.

CHAPTER 20

Lost and Found

QUESTION, HOW DO YOU LOSE A CROCK-POT? Answer is ask a teenager to put it "away." For days, I looked for one of my Crock-Pots and could not find it anywhere. I asked if anyone knew where it was, but no one did, so I went through every cabinet I thought it should be in but came up empty-handed. At this point, I was extremely frustrated. Finally, I stood at the front of the classroom and looked at all the cabinets and pretended to think like a teenager. *When they don't know where to put things, they either leave the item in plain sight or find the closest cabinet that is large enough to hold it.* I am not sure why I went to the sink first, but I did, and lo and behold, it was under the sink with all the cleaning items.

When I took my home economics classes as a student, all the kitchens were set up and equipped with all the necessities, like you would find in a home kitchen. This system did not work for me, so I organized everything by item, each in their own bin. I put all the measuring spoons in a bin, all the wooden spoons in a bin, etc. I labeled the trays and stored them in alphabetical order, which I thought would be helpful, except these days the students have a hard time spelling, and in this case, Siri *cannot* help them.

My system of organization is supposed to help the students put items back where they belong, but that doesn't always work.

One day, a student asked, "Where does this liquid measuring cup go?"

I pointed to the cabinet, just *above* the microwave labeled Liquid Measuring Cups. Later that day, I noticed it was sitting on top of the microwave all by itself, not another liquid measuring cup in sight.

A few times I have found clear custard cups stored inside my large Pyrex mixing bowls in the "teacher" cabinet. The only thing I can figure out was that the student noticed they were both clear but clearly very different in size. Apparently, the large Custard Cups label was not specific enough. I swear I can't win.

Before most labs, I have the students do a pre-lab so they can read over the recipe, assign lab tasks, and make an equipment list. In the beginning, I tell them the number of items they need on their list. I show them how to start with the ingredient section of the recipe, and as they read through each, they should be able to identify what equipment is needed for that ingredient. After the ingredient section, I explain they need to figure out the rest of the items as they read through the directions. Almost every single time, a group writes refrigerator, oven, microwave, sink, etc. as pieces of equipment. Oy vey.

Speaking of refrigerators, one day, a student asked me where to put the milk, and I said, "In the refrigerator."

She said, "Where is it?"

"They are the two huge white rectangular boxes upfront," I responded. I could not laugh because that would make her feel stupid, so I bit my lip and kept my giggles inside.

I don't know about other teachers, but finding empty milk or egg cartons in the refrigerator is now commonplace; I have no idea why, but this next story may shed some light on the problem.

A student said to me, "Where does this go?" He was holding an egg carton.

I said, "The refrigerator."

Then he said, "It's empty."

Trying to keep my face from grimacing, I said, "The trash can."

Maybe all those other empty containers went back into the refrigerator because *no one* could find a trash can even though I have ten of them in my classroom and lab area; maybe I need to have a "Snap Map" for trash cans.

CHAPTER 21

All Cracked Up

I DON'T KNOW ABOUT OTHER TEACHERS, BUT I try to train my students to use custard cups or any small bowl when cracking eggs. Of course, they ask why, so I show them a photo of a bloody egg. I took the picture at my friend's house as her husband was making a breakfast casserole. The recipe called for eight eggs, and unfortunately, the eighth egg was the bloody one; therefore, ruining the rest. He then had to go to the store to buy more eggs and start over. I thought the picture and story would be a home run for Team Custard Cup, but they struck out.

Last week, I was walking around, and I noticed that two groups had used a custard cup; however, the two eggs they needed were in the same custard cup. These groups worked directly across from each other, and I asked how both groups had the same "problem." The response was, "We just did what they did." I swear I can't make this stuff up.

One day, my Foods II class was making angel squares—a meringue dish with Oreos and pecans. I explained that the egg whites will *not* whip properly if there is *any* yolk in the whites. They seemed to understand and got to work. You know when kids are playing and then suddenly they are quiet, you wonder what just happened? Well, I had a similar situation during this lab. I saw a group of students huddled around the mixer which intrigued me because this was a group I never had to "worry" about, so I walked over.

One of them said it, "The meringue was not whipping up."

I looked in the bowl and saw that they had added the pecans way too early. I explained they didn't allow the whites to beat enough and no matter how long or hard they tried, the whites would not form properly, so I asked them to start over. They started over, and again, something went wrong, so I went to check it out.

They said, "We did it the right way, but it's not working."

I asked, "Did you get any yolk into the whites, any at all?"

"Just a little bit," said one student.

I smiled and said, "The fat from the teeny, tiny bit of yolk inhibits the meringue formation." They wanted to argue, and I said, "I am not being mean. It's all in the science."

They started again, and within a few minutes, one of the students yelled "Oh, crap!" and just as quickly, another student said, "It's okay, we used the custard cup!"

At that moment, the whole class realized the importance of custard cups and the need to make sure *no* yolk reaches the whites. I still tell that story, but unfortunately, the custard cup concept still stumps some students.

CHAPTER 22

"Where There's Smoke...or Not"

TALKING ABOUT CAREER CHOICES IS PART OF being a teacher, and this next story is by far my most memorable. In 2012, I was moved from the middle school to the high school because of some district changes. This change gave me the opportunity to work with many students I had a few years earlier, and that had many benefits, but it was not without its challenges. In one of my food classes, I had a group of four boys that I taught back in middle school. In my mind, I assumed they would behave differently now that they were older, but that was not necessarily the case. I like to refer to this group of students as "extremely active and energetic." Before I assign any labs, I review some basics—dishwashing, reading recipes, and, of course, using the right tool for the right job. It is at this point I show the students a box of wax paper and the beige bin marked PARCHMENT PAPER. I explain the difference between them—wax paper cannot go in the oven, but parchment paper can, and it aids in the cleanup process.

    The lab appeared to go smoothly until smoke began billowing out of an oven. I immediately headed toward the smoky kitchen, turned the oven off, turned the fan on, pointed to the two containers, and asked, "Which one did you use?" I knew the answer, but I wanted them to remember this. There were no more wax paper incidents the rest of "that" year.

About five years later, my home smoke detectors began beeping, and I could not turn them off. I called the nonemergency number in hopes of avoiding the big fanfare, but I lost, and they came with all bells and whistles. Of course, by the time they got there, the beeping stopped, but they insisted they check the whole house.

As we were finishing up, the cadet said to me, "Do you remember me?"

I said, "I know I had you as a student, but I can't remember when."

He responded with, "I'm Tommy. I'm the one that set the oven on fire because of the wax paper."

At that moment, his lieutenant whipped his head around and said, "You did what!"

Then he nearly passed out from laughing so hard. I told him that I think the kitchen episode only helped Tommy decide on a career path. We all laughed, and then they left. About fifteen minutes later, the detectors went off again, and, of course, another engine was dispatched, so I waited outside for them.

As they approached, one of them said, "Are you Tommy's teacher?"

I said, "I am, and I see that news travels quickly."

Tommy's story went across all forms of EMS communication devices in the district, so Tommy was the talk and laugh of the day. I have not seen Tommy since then, but I have every reason to believe he has moved easily past the cadet stage. I was proud of Tommy for being so honest in front of his boss!

CHAPTER 23

The "Wig" Raising Student

THIS NEXT STORY IS ABOUT THE STUDENT that drives you and all the other students absolutely bonkers and the entire class breathes a sigh of relief when he is absent. When he was in class, he could never stay put; maybe I should have asked, "Do you need an AirTag for your chair?" Every time this group cooked, I wondered what would happen, what would get broken, who would be meandering about the room, etc. Twice he broke a wooden spoon because he was using the bookcase as a drum, and the spoon apparently replaced the drumstick. I got better behavior from my middle school students! He was also the type of student who was very curious, and one day, he asked me very politely, "How does your wig stay on?"

I said, "It stays in place because of the band I wear under it."

Then he said, "If it's really windy, won't it blow off?"

I said, "Maybe, but I have not experienced that yet."

Then he said, "Where does the hair come from?" "How is it put together?" "Is it hot?" etc.

I finally asked, "Do you want me to take it off and show you?"

The whole class said yes, so I did. They went silent for a moment, and then a lot of questions and comments began. I had one student who wanted me to get a bright blue one and one who said I should make it a mohawk or mullet etc., but I said, "No thanks, I'll keep it basic."

A few days later, two female students came to me after class, and I asked how I could help them.

One said, "She was absent the other day…"

I asked if she needed help getting the work she missed. She said, "No, I don't care about that, but I heard you took off your wig. Would you do it for me?"

The answer, of course, was "sure." Apparently, that made her day.

CHAPTER 24

The Sin Bin

IN AUGUST OF 2021, I STARTED SEVERAL weeks of physical therapy, and that was where I became interested in hockey. I enjoyed the conversations about hockey, and without realizing it, I found myself becoming a fan...at least from the stories. What I knew about hockey was that my family and I watched the "Miracle on Ice" Olympics game in 1980 *and* that the little black "thingy" was called a puck. So forty-one years later, I finally attended my first game on New Years Eve of 2021.

Since I knew very little about hockey and absolutely nothing about the Little Caesars Arena, I found choosing seats to be somewhat overwhelming. Eventually, I selected seats in the "nosebleed" section on a corner because that would provide an overall view of everything. I later learned that area is referred to as "coaches corner," which was my first lesson, but definitely not the last.

The angle of view was not the problem because of the Jumbotron, but the walk to my seat via some steep stairs and the severe incline of the seating area caused me a lot of problems. I was so scared I would fall forward and go tumbling down several sections of spectators that I barely moved in my seat *at all*. I managed to turn my head a bit to talk to the people beside me, but even that made me nervous. I had no idea what was happening on the ice, but I didn't care because I knew I'd come back to see another game, just *not* in the upper sections. I was not scared of heights, but that night, I was almost paralyzed. I had to wait until most of the people around me left before I attempted to get out of my seat and head back down the stairs. Once I got to my car, I could finally breathe. From that point forward, I was in love with the game, and the rest is history. This is the journal entry I wrote the next day, January 1, 2022.

> *That will definitely not be my one and only game :) I had no idea that hockey was so entertaining—did not know that "Sweet Caroline" was a sing-along, and I had never seen bubble hockey. How can I climb into trees, walk across 2×4 boards held together by ropes hanging from a cable, zip across a cable, go sky high and deep beneath the water, but nearly have a heart attack from sheer fear while getting to my seat? I was scared to death and sat there like a piece of petrified wood dreading the climb down! The seats had a great view, but those stairs… not happening again! Next game will probably be in the "100" level! I can see why it's a popular sport—the game pace is fast and intense, but there was only one fight though—I thought there would be more.*
> *Happy New Year to me!*

I continued to learn as much as I could and watched as many games as I could—which was a lot. What I didn't really think about was how positively my new interest would impact my relationships with my students.

The first day of the second semester of 2022, I asked each class if anyone played hockey. The students who raised their hand were told they did not have to do any work for the semester—they would get an "A" just because they played hockey. They cheered, but then I had to say "Just kidding." The three players who raised their hand more or less became my "coaches."

One of our first serious hockey conversations was about an NHL player who I would eventually learn was "usually" in trouble. As a newbie, I didn't understand how the hockey world worked, so I was learning much more than just the game. My coaches came into class on a regular basis asking me things like, "Did you see that hit last night by...," "Have you heard about...," and my favorite question was, "Are you coming to our hockey game tomorrow night?" I did not attend many games, but I always asked "How'd it go?"

In case you haven't noticed, I like humor, especially when it comes to my students, so I couldn't help myself when I asked them this joke, "Why are the corners of the rink rounded instead of ninety degrees?"

They didn't question my authenticity because I was very serious and I was, after all, learning the ropes. They proceeded to say things like, that would be unsafe, people would end up jabbing sticks, breaking sticks, and most likely several fights would break out. Then I told them, "If they were ninety degrees, the ice would melt." I couldn't fool them much after that, but that did not keep them from trying.

As a matter of fact, they were quite good at trying to bargain their way out of doing classwork. One day, they noticed there was a pile of dirty dishes and a basket of clean rags that needed folding. They said they would do the dishes and fold the rags if I didn't make them do the "worksheet." I "let them" squirm a bit to see how far they would try before I agreed—it was extremely fun for me—so I said, "If it's not to my satisfaction, I'll call a penalty and you'll end up in the sin bin."

By the end of class, I had clean dishes and folded towels. They bragged to their friends about how they "got out of" an assignment because they convinced me to let them do the dishes instead of the work. What they didn't know was that the assignment wasn't going to be graded. They never knew that until the following year when they stopped by to see what classes I was teaching because they wanted to take another class with me. Unfortunately, the scheduling didn't work out; however, they continued to visit me on a regular basis, especially when they heard I had made ice cream or dirt cake, but there is more to this story.

I had a student with autism in that same class who would seldom engage with me or other students. Then I learned he was a huge Red Wings fan, and a connection was made. I went on Amazon and bought a hockey box for kids, with the Pittsburgh Penguins and the Philadelphia Flyers. It had a vinyl rink, nets, and players.

One day, I got the box and said, "Would you please set this up because I have a few questions I need you to explain."

He didn't ask any questions and got right to work. I asked him to show me the basics—what the lines mean, what's a face-off, what's a penalty, what's offsides, etc. After my "lesson," he said, "You know this would have been a lot more fun if the Red Wings were one of the teams." I chuckled and told him to contact Amazon to make a complaint, and he grinned.

I have had the pleasure of working with him in three different classes over a two-year period, and what a difference hockey had made in our relationship. Where he was once disengaged, he is now very engaged…by giving me the daily hockey report. If I am not in his line of sight when he comes in, he tracks me down and immediately starts explaining what I "missed" last night regarding the game. I don't think I would have ever connected with him if it weren't for hockey.

CHAPTER 25

Part 1
Sewcial

BEING QUARANTINED FOR MONTHS IS NOT SOMETHING I put on my bucket list, but nevertheless, it happened, and it was quite the experience. Prior to the pandemic, I had been struggling on several personal and professional levels, so being forced to slow down and think deeply about my life and where it was heading was something I needed very badly and didn't even know it. The pandemic forced families and individuals to navigate obstacles and challenges that were not on anyone's radar pre-pandemic; for example, I never thought I would be teaching students online via Zoom and realizing that might mean there would be no more snow days. Ugh. I also never imagined having to set my alarm clock to make sure I got to the grocery store at 6:00 a.m. in order to purchase a dozen eggs and toilet paper, which reminded me of the toilet paper bouquet that I saw on FaceBook—just one of the creative and hilarious moments that lightened the whole situation. Who knew that toilet paper would be such a hot commodity that toilet paper bouquets would be preferable to flowers?

I am grateful that my family and I did not experience the loss of loved ones, and for those who did, I would never make light of those situations. There were sad stories hitting the news headlines, and there were some uplifting and funny ones as well. One of my favorite headlines was from CNN: WILD GOATS TAKE OVER WELSH

Town amid Coronavirus Lockdown. I laughed trying to envision goats running amok. It was not a big deal but one of those little bright moments.

The quarantine mandate was basically lifesaving for me. The four to five years preceding the pandemic were very difficult for me, and I was hanging on by a thread, no pun intended. Knowing I had to get up each day and head to school provided a sense of normalcy for me; however, by the time we were in quarantine, I was exhausted and feeling less than productive.

My mom was an excellent seamstress and a *big* fan of the Stretch and Sew patterns, and I have the elementary school pictures to prove it! I was not ashamed of the clothes she made, except for the homemade bathing suits, and I was very excited when she made my new outfit from the fabric I had selected—purple paisley stretch. However, the look of paisley-print stretchy bell bottom pants was not a good look for a chubby kid. Luckily, the school pictures were only headshots.

At the age of ten, I asked my mom to teach me how to use the sewing machine, but she felt she would not be the best teacher, so she signed me up for sewing lessons. The first item I made was a summer dress made from Holly Hobbie fabric. The pattern required a zipper closure which can be tricky, but apparently not for me. My teacher told my mom that she had never seen a student do such a good job on their first attempt. Because of my mom's desire to help me develop my sewing talent, I was able to start my sewing journey, and I have not stopped.

Once I entered middle school, I took my first home economics class. At one point during the sewing unit, I convinced my mom to help my teacher, Mrs. Anderson, because she couldn't help everyone, and so between the three of us, my seventh-grade sewing unit was a success. From that point forward, all my home ec teachers allowed me to do whatever project I wanted. Never once did I think that my sewing skills would help save the world during a pandemic.

One of my colleagues has two sisters that worked in the women's health medical field, and she reached out to see if I would help her to make masks for them. Of course, I said yes, and the sewing frenzy began. I used quite a bit of my fabric stash, but I did purchase U of M and Spartan fabric specifically for our project. Throughout the quarantine, my colleagues—past and present—joined together to make one hundred-plus masks in a matter of days. This is a journal entry from April 7, 2020:

> *I have really had fun doing this b/c it allows me to be creative and serve a purpose. Amy and I were talking about how this chunk of time we've been given is a once-in-a-lifetime gift; there will never be another chunk of time like this where we don't have to worry about school but can spend time w/ family w/o worrying about family being all over the place. Having your kids in one place can either be a gift or a curse for parents of children and teens* (Amy has 3 teenagers).

I am an introvert, so staying home to sew was like manna from heaven. I spent my day interacting with each of my classes for a short period of time and then went to work on the masks. When possible, I put a little twist into my mask making in hopes of helping the recipients laugh even if it's just for a moment. For many masks, I used food-theme fabric on the mouth pattern piece. Once I ran out of popcorn fabric, I used my pretzel-, candy-, and coffee-themed fabric. Apparently, the staff loved these and got a kick out of my idea.

At one point, Amy's two oldest children began making masks, and I teased her that she was breaking child labor laws because she was not paying them. They, however, were savvy businesspeople and decided to sell the masks because Amy and I were donating the masks we made. She told them they had to make fifty masks before she would post them on Facebook for purchase.

As the mask making continued, so did our text messaging. This is just one of the text messages I received from Amy regarding our mask donation: *Marlena called my mom on the way home from the hospital today, things are pretty bad. Body bags…lots of friends exhausted! Said to relay how much the masks mean!* Amy sent me another text about her other sister: *Noelle said the doctors were crying when she gave them the bag of masks! We are serving a higher purpose, friend. Hugs to you.* These texts brought tears to my eyes because I knew I made the right choice to sew masks for donations instead of spending the time to work on my own projects.

In addition to the masks, Amy was asked if we could make surgical caps; of course, we both said yes. Amy attempted to make a cap, but something went terribly wrong, and she asked me to fix it. I made a few adjustments to the construction directions, and soon I was making caps and Amy was making masks. The doctors got a real kick out of the reversible caps I made because I used beer and wine fabric for one side but left the other side "respectable." Again, just a little thing I could do to make someone smile. Here is another text I received from Amy: *Marlena loves the caps! She took masks yesterday, and people were grabbing them like hot cakes! She said if we can do a big amount of caps, they would love it!* Amy shared that her family was always saying, "Amy teaches reproductive health, Noelle helps them through the pregnancy, and Marlena catches them at the end!"

Not long into the mask frenzy, I suggested we call ourselves "The Masked Seamstresses." We never did, but who cares, because we had a great time contributing our time and materials for people on the front lines. If you are a quilter or know a quilter, then you know how important our fabric stash is to us, and you surely know the phrase, "She who dies with the most fabric wins!" Well, I am not going to win because I depleted my stash for the masks and have *not* replenished it…yet.

Part 2
Distancing

The week before spring break of 2020, our school district went virtual and was hoping to return after break, but we all know the rest of that story. As I embarked on my first virtual educational experience, I had to think about how to approach my assignments because I did not want to add any additional stress to my students' load, but I wanted to hold them accountable. We were required to hold a Zoom meeting for the first fifteen minutes of class, and then the remaining thirty minutes were to provide time for the work to be completed. We have a block schedule, so we only "saw" our students every other day.

At the time, my Foods II class was preparing to turn in their Home Cooking Project, which was very detailed and time-consuming; therefore, I saw no need to add more work for these students. Of course, the students who had not even started the project were grateful to "be off the hook"—for that assignment anyway.

My Foods I class had just finished a project, and I was not planning on assigning another one, so their assignments were based on my idea of COP—choice of points. I felt my students would benefit the most if they were able to take ownership of their assignments by selecting the tasks that worked the best for them in their situation. The students were required to earn fifteen points per week and were given three categories from which to choose: 5, 10, or 15 points. Some examples of assignments were as follows: five-point categories focused on textbook objective-type answers; ten-point categories were practical, such as cleaning and organizing the refrigerator and pantry; the fifteen-point category required the student to plan and prepare dinner for the family. The meal had to include three items—excluding beverages and dessert—with one of them being made from a recipe, the table had to be set properly, and they would have to enforce the No Phone Zone at the table.

I can't recall all the recipes that were used or remember all the summaries I read, but I did hear a lot of feedback through our daily Zoom meetings. Students appeared to be happy because they were able to have choices. I love to assign projects because they force students to tap into their higher-order thinking skills (HOTS) instead of just prepping for a written test. Students would have to demonstrate employability skills, such as time-management, resource management, and problem-solving skills in order to accomplish their tasks. I used the same system for my child development class and for the Foods II students who did not complete the Home Cooking Project.

My family and relationships class had one required assignment—they were to keep a journal during the quarantine so they could "see" how all their relationships were impacted. When we had our Zoom meetings, many of them complained about not being able to see their friends, go to prom, and or being able to graduate in the traditional fashion. I had several seniors in this class, and they were stressing out over what their first year of college would look like. We used our Zoom time to talk through some of these concerns and what could be done to help reduce their anxiety. I was basically "there" for them in whatever capacity they needed. I thoroughly enjoyed reading the journal entries because I gained new insight into situations I had never thought about. I am single and an introvert, so being quarantined did not cause the same stress for me as it did for many of my students. Reading about what they were experiencing was good for me because it helped me sympathize.

CHAPTER 26

Rewind or Unwind?

LAST SPRING 2023, OUR DISTRICT ANNOUNCED WE were "upgrading" from a PC-operating system to a MacBook-operating system. When I heard about the technology upgrade, I wanted to retire on the spot. We were given about two weeks to remove, upload, etc. anything from our hard drives to Google Drive. I followed all the directions, but something went wrong, and I lost about seven thousand files, and the tears began, literally.

In 1994, I started my second year with the Henrico County Public Schools, and that year, our district, which was an entire county, was providing iBooks to each student. I thought that was very cool and forward-thinking, but many of the "older" teachers decided to retire. I was befuddled because I didn't understand why a new computer would cause someone to "be done." Thirty-one years later, I completely understand.

So when people ask me when I am retiring, I say "I don't know" because as long as I can still put the students first and continue to build relationships, I might find myself teaching for another thirty years and writing the sequel to this book, *There's* Still *No Prereq for Home Ec*. So the question is, do I rewind or unwind?

CHAPTER 27

The Misfits

THESE ARE MY STORIES THAT REALLY DON'T really fit anywhere else.

I am pretty accident-prone, and a few years ago, I started my first day of school by being taken out of the building by the EMS. As usual, my floors had been waxed over the summer; and this time, they were extremely shiny and slick. So when I bent over in my chair to open a file drawer, the chair went in one direction and I went the other. Of course that particular day, I decided to wear a dress. Luckily I was able to push it back in place before anyone saw me. The funniest part of the whole thing was that the students hadn't seen or realized what happened. It wasn't until someone said, "Where did she go?"

I said, "*I'm down here*," raised my hand, and waved.

*****

On New Year's Day 2012, I was bitten by a cat and ended up in the hospital for a week, right before school started again. On my first day back to class, with my hand bandaged and my arm in a sling, the first question I heard was, "Are we going to cook today?"

I thought, *Do I laugh, or do I cry?*

*****

Prior to getting my wig, I would have never agreed to have a whipped cream pie thrown in my face, but I agreed to it this year. It was the last lunch period and I didn't get many throwers; however, that did not keep one of my "challenging" students from bumming a dollar off someone else, throwing the pie, and taking a picture. I haven't seen it on Instagram, so I think I'm safe.

*****

While teaching interior design, I had the students measure their bedroom, furniture and all, and draw it to scale on graph paper. I explained that each square equals one foot, and I showed them some examples of what the end result should look like. I had one student who could not grasp the concept of the graph paper no matter how many times and ways I tried to help her. When she turned in her assignment, her queen-size bed measured fifteen feet by twenty feet. I wondered, *Where does she buy her sheets?*

For a middle school interior design project, the students were creating furniture arrangements for various rooms, and one student placed a grand piano in the master bedroom.

I asked, "Why is there a grand piano in the master bedroom?"

She said, "There's too much space and it looks empty."

"Yesterday we talked about doors. Do you remember what I said?"

"To place furniture so it's not hit by the door. That is why I put it *here*." She pointed to the piano in the middle of the floor space.

"That is true, but I also talked about door sizes. How will it get through the doorway?"

With a little sheepish grin on her face, she said, "Oh, I didn't think of that."

*****

Several years ago, one of my classes was working quietly on an assignment when I heard a "slapping" noise, so I looked up. What I saw were two girls slapping each other without saying a word. I immediately got out of my chair, yelling, "What the f—— are you doing?" and stepped in to separate them. Of course, the students could not believe I dropped the f-bomb. I felt really bad about it, so I sent my principal an email to explain that there had been a fight in my classroom that day. Well, at parent-teacher conferences that night, he walked up to me with a very serious expression and said, "I didn't know you dropped the f-bomb today." I was speechless but began to dig my way out of the hole I was in. Then he smiled and said, "One of the administrators told me what happened. You're not in trouble."

"Very funny," I said and smiled.

*****

A few years ago, my health class was working on an e-assignment about emotions. The assignment was from a personal perspective, meaning the answers were subjective. As I was looking over the answers on Luke's assignment, I noticed that he put down "postpartum depression." I was concerned, so I went to him and said, "Luke, how often do you experience postpartum depression?"

He said, "What's that?"

"That is what some women experience after giving birth."

He said, "Oh," as his face turned red.

"So if you're going to cut and paste answers, at least read them first." I shook my head slightly as I walked away.

*****

Recently I was folding kitchen towels during a lab and one of my students asked, "Why are you folding the towels?"

I said, "Because they won't fold themselves. Don't you fold your towels?"

"No, we hang them up."

I said, "Well, I am sure you have folded towels somewhere in the house."

"Well, I've never folded them. I've only hung them."

Since he was wearing his JROTC camouflage uniform, I said, "You know you can't take your mom to boot camp to fold your towels, right?"

He said, "I'm not going to boot camp. I'm going to shoe camp."

"What's that?"

"It's easier than boot camp."

I said, "Good one," with a smile on my face as I told him to fold the rest of the towels and put them in the drawer.

*****

Oddly enough it was his group that used the broom to sweep the cake mix that had gotten on the counter. I suppose in his defense he did say, "You told us to sweep the counter." Sometimes, I have no words; and other times, I have some words I shouldn't use!

*****

When I was teaching sixth grade at Three Fires Middle School, I had to do some bribing. Clearly bribing is not a great method to encourage good behavior, but they were squirmy and noisy, so I had to think outside the box. It was the last class of the day and they were ready to leave the building, like Elvis. I am not sure why I did this but I started to dance the waltz by myself. Well, this got everyone's attention, and for about thirty seconds, they were quiet as a church mouse. When I finished, the questions started coming.

"What are you doing?"

"What kind of dance is that?"

"Don't you need a partner?" With a slight smile, I confirmed "Yes, but Tom Cruise is unavailable."

They stayed focused and on task for the rest of the class period. The next day, when they came in, someone asked, "What dance are you doing today?"

I said, "You really want me to dance again?"

In unison, I heard "Yes."

So I said, "Okay, at the end of class, I will do another dance as long as you're working and listening." At the end of the class, I showed them the "sprinkler." The next day, I showed them the "shopping cart" and so forth. I think there were about five or six dances altogether—waltz, cha-cha, Charleston, sprinkler, shopping cart, snorkel. Some wanted me to do the worm, but I *refused* to get on my stomach and *inch* my way across the floor. For the rest of the quarter, the DOD ("dance of the day") became a daily activity, and I let the class decide which one they wanted me to do, which was usually the *shopping cart*. I don't think this strategy would ever find its way into an official manuscript of classroom management strategies, but it worked for me.

ACKNOWLEDGMENTS

I WANT TO THANK THE PEOPLE WHO cheered me on as I took my writing journey. Debbie Miller, friend and former colleague, was my partner in crime when we both taught at Three Fires Middle School. Debbie and my two aunts were my book reviewers, but I believe my aunts were biased, so I relied on Debbie to "give it to me straight," which she did. I have talked to my Aunt Sue every Saturday morning for years, and she has listened to my stories, my frustrations, and my ideas for additional chapters. Last but not least is my Aunt Gloria. She has been my biggest fan, which is funny because she is only 4'9", but she has the spirit and laughter the size of the jolly green giant. When she read the sample chapters I sent, she said, "Gloria, I hope to live long enough to be able to have a leather-bound book of your story. I truly think this is a winner. So proud of you." Then recently, she said, "I would love to buy the first one, autographed copy by the author!" Talk about being under pressure! She just turned ninety-six, and I hope she does get the first copy, but there is *no way* she's paying for it. Thanks to all of you for your help, your guidance, and your ability to laugh with me.

ABOUT THE AUTHOR

Gloria Humphreys has been a home economics/Family and Consumer Sciences (FCS) educator since 1992. During her tenure, she has had the opportunity to work with middle and high school age students in various capacities. She has taught sixth-grade exploratory; teen living; independent living; interior design; education for employment; child development; Nutrition and Culinary Arts I and II; reading; customs, cultures, and cuisines; creative living; consumer economics; family and relationships; career exploration; careers, money & more!, health; and clothing construction classes. In addition to teaching, she also sponsored the FHA/FCCLA program at the middle school level, was the head coach for girls' soccer, the assistant coach for girls' basketball, was the yearbook and school newspaper sponsors, and the coordinator for the Education for Employment program. She won the Teacher of the Year Award from Byrd Middle School for 1999–2002 and was nominated for Teacher of the Year for Howell High School in 2020 and 2024. In 2016, she was a workshop speaker during the Michigan Family and Consumer Sciences Conference in Frankenmuth, Michigan. She is a member of the Michigan Association of Family and Consumer Sciences (MIFCS) and the American Association of Family and Consumer Sciences (AAFCS). In addition to her bachelor degree she has an M.A. in Family Studies from Western Michigan University. Prior to becoming a teacher she held several retail jobs, including Clinique cosmetics where she was a counter manager. For almost fifty years, she has been an avid seamstress and quilter and has spent many summers working at her family's business, Springer's Homemade Ice Cream.

www.ingramcontent.com/pod-product-compliance
Lightning Source LLC
Chambersburg PA
CBHW032308141224
18930CB00062B/442